CHURCH
PLANTING
MADE EASY

SAMUEL UKOMADU, PhD

WESTBOW®
PRESS
A DIVISION OF THOMAS NELSON
& ZONDERVAN

WestBow Press books may be ordered through booksellers or by contacting:

WestBow Press
A Division of Thomas Nelson & Zondervan
1663 Liberty Drive
Bloomington, IN 47403
www.westbowpress.com
1 (866) 928-1240

ISBN: 978-1-4908-2712-4 (sc)
ISBN: 978-1-4908-2713-1 (hc)
ISBN: 978-1-4908-2711-7 (e)

Library of Congress Control Number: 2014903464

Printed in the United States of America.

WestBow Press rev. date: 03/05/2014

Contents

INTRODUCTION ix

Leadership in Church Planting xiv
Leadership Styles xv
The United States Population xvi
Builders...xvii
Boomers...xvii
Busters and Millennials..xx
Urban Church Planting...xx
Socio-Political Factors Affecting Church Planting....................xxii
Incorporation..xxiv
State Tax-Exempt Status xxiv
Taxpayer Identification Number...xxiv
Mailing Address xxv
Telephone Service... xxv
Government Regulations xxv

CHAPTER 1: CHURCH PLANT UNDER REVIEW 1

The History of Church Planting...3
The Need for Church Planting..6
The Impact of Culture in Church Planting......................................9
Church Growth 12
The Church Planting Process 13

CHAPTER 2: BIBLICAL AND THEOLOGICAL APPROACH.. 17

The Formation of the Church..17
The Church and its Effect on Modern Society 20
The Plan of Salvation 22
Chaplaincy 24
Nationally Appointed US Missionaries for Chaplaincy............26
Chi Alpha Campus Ministries, USA 26
Church Development..29
Nationally Appointed US Missionaries for Church
Development 30
Intercultural Ministries..30
Summer Volunteer 31
One- to Two-Year Missionary Associates 32
RV Volunteers...32
MAPS Construction and Evangelism Teams.............................33
Teen Challenge International, USA 33
Youth Alive...35

CHAPTER 3: REKINDLING THE VISION 38

The Coach and the Church Planter..44
Ten Reasons to Consider a New Work Coach............................47
Desirable Characteristics of Coaches 48
Church Planting Models 49
Natural Birth..49
The Adoption Method 51
The Implantation Model..51
Introduction to Multi-Congregational Churches......................53

CHAPTER 4: REDISCOVERING CHURCH PLANTING 61

The Church and the Church Planter...63

Research Implications...65

Rejection...66

Discouragement...68

Burnout...68

Finances..69

Spiritual Warfare...69

Research Applications 70

Conclusions..71

Future Research...72

Works Cited 75

Appendix...81

Introduction

In recent time, urban centers have grown at a greater rate than suburban areas. This increase in the urban environment has produced new demographic and cultural shifts. Many events have shown that North America is now the largest mission field in the English-speaking world and the third-largest after China and India.[1] Today, a missionary does not need to climb a mountain or cross a deep sea to reach a mission field that is both challenging and promising. One of the leading evangelical churches in the United States of America (the Assemblies of God) has created a department called Home Missions.[2] The department reaches out to a segment of American society with the intent of bringing its people back to the original salvation plan of God.

To a large extent, in this dissertation, we have analyzed church planting as it relates to the Assemblies of God Church in the United States. To achieve this goal, we have taken into account the demographics of church planting for the past two and a half years. Church planting can be defined as an effort by an individual or group of persons who feel the call of God in their lives to evangelize and start a new church.

According to Boydston, "Church planting is one of the means through which disciples are gathered into viable Christian

---

[1]   David Yount, *The Future of Christian Faith in America* (New York: Macmillan Press, 2004), 8.

[2]   "Enrichment," *A Journal for Pentecostal Ministry* (Winter 2006), 18.

communities."[3] In many ways, the new congregation is much more like the initial community of disciples Jesus gathered than established modern churches. This is not to say established churches are any less representative of the church; rather, the new congregation has a fresh sense of mission and new form of ministry.

Luke made it clear that after the outpouring of the Holy Spirit at Pentecost, fellowship groups contributed to the massive wave of conversions to Christ. In Acts 2:41–42, Luke wrote, "Those who believed what Peter said were baptized and added to the church—about three thousand in all. They joined with the other believers and devoted themselves to the apostles' teaching and fellowship, sharing in the Lord's Supper and in prayer." The establishment of such groups—churches—was repeated numerous times throughout Acts and was a major aspect of the apostolic mission. The apostles did not just proclaim the gospel and perform great signs in the name of Christ; they also established churches. Peter Wagner drew a comparison between these early churches and modern church plantings, writing, "The single most effective evangelistic methodology under heaven is planting new churches."[4]

In the field of church planting, the church planter is defined as a person—national or foreigner—who sows the gospel seed in such a way that a New Testament church comes to life and grows. The growing number of immigrants in to the United States have increased the country's cultural and demographic diversity. These immigrants bring significant changes that affect Christianity and the church.

The church has developed numerous strategies with the hope of reaching this burgeoning population. Indeed, it would be foolish for the church not to adapt and respond to the needs

---

[3]   Bradley L. Boydston, *Getting Started, A Church Planting Handbook for Laypeople* (Turlock, California: Bradley L. Boydston, 2002), 4.

[4]   Peter Wagner, *Church Planting for Greater Harvest* (Glendale, California: Regal Books, 1990), 12.

of this population. Modern society, marked by increasing levels of diversity and cynicism, demands new styles of evangelism. In some churches, the music has changed. Mostly contemporary songs are sung in the church, and Christian music is changing fast. Audiovisual equipment is prominent; projectors and even satellite television, among other audiovisual aids, are now prevalent in American churches. A new position in the ministry is the media minister, who develops and directs church media. Indeed, pastoral leadership and training are more necessary now than ever before.

Research Problem

According to David T. Olson in his book *The American Church in Crisis,* there are 220 million people in North America who do not know Christ as their Savior. There is a great need for church planters in this vast mission field. A large proportion of the aforementioned population lives in urban areas and the rural countryside, which are areas that typically fall outside the existing evangelical comfort zone. Church planting calls for a basic biblical attitude that must be internalized into the personal fabric of the church planter. Philippians 2:5 stated, "Let this mind be in you which was in Christ Jesus." Romans 12:2 invoked a similar message: "Let God transform you inwardly by a complete change of your mind."

Olson suggested that the modern United States—particularly in urban areas—is a fertile ground for church planting. Church planters require a strategy to reach this population, as many church planters have voiced concerns over their ability to form successful new congregations. The goal of this study is to develop a strategy that will allow twenty-first-century church planters to successfully plant churches in the urban United States.

Our present society is marked by a high level of religious apathy, which is demonstrated by low attendance at church and worship sessions. According to Olson, on average, only 17.5 percent of Americans attended a worship service at a Christian church on any given weekend in 2005. In 1990, that percentage was over 20 percent.[5] In the face of these discouraging statistics, some observers believe God has prompted Christians to go back to the basic principle of evangelism. New church plants are springing up all over the United States, and God is raising an increasing number of church planters during this time.

Modern society is increasingly interested in luxury and excesses and holds little interest in religion. Some people have even developed their own unique religions—mishmashes of different religious performances. These tendencies have promoted widespread confusion. Love for God has grown cold in the hearts of many people in the United States. Due to these problems, there is a need to develop leaders who will be involved in church planting to bring the purpose of God into fruition.

The Pentecostal and Evangelical churches have their differences. However, both denominations seek to achieve the same objective—to serve God with utmost obedience by evangelizing to the world. Without question, there is a general consensus among all denominations that preaching the gospel to all humanity is God's injunction to which all Christians must abide. This message of the kingdom must be preached to every creature to make God's plan for salvation complete before the return of Jesus Christ.

Peter Wagner is a renowned Christian leader and a church planter. As a leader in the field of church planting, he confirmed the need for church planting in this current era. Further, he identified the core values of church planting as character, evidence of being called into ministry, self-awareness, commitment to theology and the kingdom of God, worship, relationship with the community, training, and missions both home and abroad.

---

[5] David T. Olsen, *The American Church in Crisis* (Grand Rapids, Michigan: Zondervan, 2008), 28.

The American church is in crisis. This declaration might not square with some evidence; every Sunday in some cities, the roads become clogged with thousands heading to mega-churches. There are numerous notable mega-churches in the United States: Lakewood Church in Houston, Texas; Potter's House in Dallas, Texas; Saddleback Community Church in Orange County, California; the Life Church in Oklahoma City, Oklahoma; and Salem Baptist Church in Chicago, Illinois. These are just a few. However, research has shown that the combined weekly attendance of the ten fastest-growing churches in America is only 153,232 people. Further, the top one hundred fastest-growing Pentecostal churches increased their numbers by only 141,148 attendees in 2007. In a study released in May 2007, the Barna Group reported that only 43 percent of Americans attend church each week.

Ultimately, comparing the US population that attends church with the population at large demonstrates that the church is in crisis. Every Sunday, many Americans do not attend church services. On Sundays, most people in the United States wash their cars, mow their lawns, sleep, and enjoy leisure time. As the American population continues to grow, attending church continues to drop in popularity. Statistics have shown that if this trend continues, by 2050, the percentage of Americans attending church will be much lower. There is the urgent need for evangelicals and other church leaders to increase their church-planting efforts; otherwise, the church may become extinct.

Strategic leadership is key to successful urban church planting in North America. A strategy for training leaders is therefore necessary to accomplish the purpose and plan of God in this generation. According to Col W. Michael Guillot, USAF, strategic leadership is the ability of an experienced, senior leader who has the wisdom and vision to create and execute plans and make consequential decisions in the volatile, uncertain, complex, and ambiguous strategic environment.

Strategic leadership entails making decisions across different cultures, agencies, agendas, personalities, and desires. It requires the devising of plans that are feasible, desirable, and acceptable to one's organization and partners—whether joint, interagency, or multinational. Strategic leadership demands the ability to make sound, reasoned decisions—specifically, consequential decisions with grave implications. The strategy is the plan; strategic leadership is the thinking and decision-making required to develop an effective plan.

The church planter is a strategic leader who needs to be well-equipped with complex training that affords him or her the opportunity to strategically develop a plan of evangelism and successfully reach out to diverse cultures in the twenty-first-century church. There are some sociopolitical and spiritual problems to be overcome; therefore, a comprehensive plan needs to be mapped out to accomplish the set goal. Training in computer operation may be required, since today's worshippers are exposed to modern technology in worship, such as beaming the preaching and worship songs during church sessions on a projector screen. Strategically, the church planter must reach out to the diverse population in North America.

Leadership in Church Planting

The importance of leadership in church planting cannot be overemphasized. A church is only as good as its planter. The church planter must have a vision and the passion to pursue the vision. Vision allows church planters to push through problems. Vision provides the energy for the effort. Without vision, the passion leaks, church production falls, and its people scatter.

Jesus was a great leader who led by example. This style of leadership will be a guide for anyone who envisions planting a church. The church planter must possess a character trait that followers must emulate; church followers should be able to see Jesus through the planter. According to Matthew 28:19 (KJV), Jesus gave the instruction, "Go ye therefore, and teach all nations, baptizing them in the name of the Father, and of the Son, and of the Holy Ghost."

As the disciples planted churches, Jesus planned that each church would reproduce another church. Acts 1:8 advises, "But you shall receive power when the Holy Ghost has come upon you; and you shall be witnesses to Me in Jerusalem, and in all Judea and Samaria, and to the end of the earth." Jesus understood the need for a church plant.

Leadership Styles

There are four potential styles of leadership that a church planter can have. They can possess directing, strategic, team-building, and operational styles of leadership. Directing leaders tend to focus on the big picture; they are motivational leaders who focus people's attention on their visions for the future. They are most likely to exhibit biblical values; however, those who follow directing leaders often struggle with serving and exhibiting loving hearts. Directing leaders, with their aggressive nature and excessive zeal, may hurt some of the very people they wish to help.

Strategic leaders analyze information, evaluate options, and recommend the most effective courses of action. They are the strongest types of leaders when it comes to faith, maturity, and exhibiting biblical wisdom. However, they are prone to difficulties with their tempers and strong speech. They become so passionate that they may lose patience with those people who hold different opinions. Strategic leaders make decisions that affect a lot of people, commit more resources, and have wider-ranging consequences on both time and space than the operational and direct leaders.

While team-building leaders fail to outshine their fellow leaders in any particular character quality, they are very relational and able to get people excited about their roles in pursuing the vision. However, they are often inefficient communicators of transformational or strategic principles.

Operational leaders develop systems that promote the efficiency and effectiveness of an organization, maximizing the flow of information and services. Operational leaders are weaker than their colleagues when it comes to their ability to control their tempers, their godly demeanors, their relationships to servant-hood, and their teaching abilities. Operational leaders focus on making the process work to such a degree that it sometimes causes them to become overtly frustrated with the efforts of others. The operational leaders deal with complex issues, great uncertainty, and often come out with great, unexpected results. This leadership find themselves influencing people through policymaking and systems integration more than the strategic leaders.

According to Peter Wagner, the church is a reflection of the pastor. In view of the new worship culture, one begins to imagine what kind of pastoral leadership would satisfy the need created by this diversified group of Christians. This study would examine the dynamics for the production of a pastor that would function effectively in this kind of environment. Strategies would be developed for reaching out to the emerging population of worshippers that includes the young and the elderly.

The United States Population

The current generational mix in the United States has called for different styles of worship. US citizens fall into a number of broad generational groups that include the Builders, Boomers, Busters, Millennials, and Babies. According to Stetzer, the Builders are those people who were born before 1946. At the turn of the millennium, there were more than 50 million of these people in the United States and eight million in Canada. Next, the Boomers were born during the two decades following World War II. As of 2000, the Boomers comprised the largest single segment of the population, with more than 70 million in the United States and eight million in Canada. Following the Boomers were the Busters, who were born between 1965 and 1976. There are 30 million Busters in the United States, while seven million reside in Canada. The Millennials, the following generational group, were born from 1977 to 1994. At the beginning of the twenty-first century, there were more than 70 million Millennials.

Builders

Builders dominate most churches. As a result, church attendance in the United States skews older, though some young people have been successfully integrated into the church. Builders are marked by their individualistic behavior and pride themselves on their success and hard work.[6]

Boomers

Boomers comprise the post-World War II generation (born between 1946 and 1964). In the last two decades, the majority of new churches tended to reach out to this group. Stetzer argued that the style and organization of "Boomer churches" tends to look very different from those founded by Builders. He noted numerous factors that differentiate those in the Boomer generation, particularly in their spiritual lives:

---

[6] Ibid.

Table 1

The Common Characteristics of Boomers
i   Boomers are the first generation raised with absentee fathers.
ii Boomers are the first generation whose grandparents had significant input in their lives.
iii Boomers are the most educated generation in history.
iv Boomers were raised with extreme affluence and great opportunities.
v   Boomers have less purchasing power than their parents at each stage of adulthood.
vi Boomers were raised under the threat of nuclear war.
vii Boomers were the first generation to be reared with television as a significant parenting tool.[7]

---

[7]   Ibid., 107.

Table 2

	More Characteristics of Boomers
i	Boomers are open to spiritual experience.
ii	Boomers' Bible teaching emphasizes practical living.
iii	Boomers place a healthy emphasis on relationships.
iv	Boomers have fewer titles and less formal in their behaviors.
v	Boomers understand the new family in America.
vi	Boomers share their faith by what they say and do.
vii	Boomers recognize the ability of women.
viii	Boomers place an emphasis on worship.
ix	Boomers have a high tolerance for diversity.
x	Boomers are action-oriented.[8]

---

[8] Ibid., 109.

Busters and Millennials

The Busters and the Millennials comprise the next generation of worshippers. The church must adopt new approaches in order to meet these generational groups. Younger generations in the United States are marked by increasing levels of ethnic and religious diversity. Generational changes call for diverse church planting in order to reach these populations. Churches emerge either in suburbs, villages, or small towns. Generational differences affect the location and efficacy of a church. Most church planting in the 1990s depended on large churches sending out teams of people to establish new churches in a relatively local vicinity; as a result, church planting was an overwhelmingly local phenomenon.

Urban Church Planting

Numerous urban church planting efforts have been made over the years, but many of these have failed, because those involved in the planting effort were unwilling or unable to grapple with the urban cultures into which they planted and tried to import a model of church that did not fit the local culture. Even those churches that have appeared to succeed are typically marked by a failure to develop indigenous leadership, which has resulted in dependence on outside support and an inability to penetrate the local community.

There are hurdles to overcome in planting a church in an urban community with a diverse group of people. Many urban communities are generally suspicious of newcomers in general— especially those from a different racial group or socioeconomic class. This is particularly true with respect to church planting incomers; community suspicion can take time to overcome. The urban community recognizes that many of these churches and other social groups do not last for long.

The demands of urban communities weigh heavy on church planters. Countless social needs place additional demands on church planters. These planters shoulder additional burdens and must be wary of burnout. Further, adding new members to a church plant—the obvious goal of church planting—tends to increase the demands on church planters rather than dispersing the load.

Urban communities tend to be culturally diverse, fitting into countless demographic categories. Therefore, church planters must also be aware of cultural circumstances and issues. This is crucial for church planting in any area but is particularly important and complex in many urban communities, where shifting populations, the interplay between different ethnic communities and subcultures, changing dynamics across generations, and other factors demand more of church planters. The diversity of the population to be served raises important questions about the design and implementation of church planting efforts.

The growth of minority ethnic groups and lifestyles in urban America means that the church must develop new congregations to meet the needs of these subcultures. Likewise, the church needs to recognize that even among English-speaking people, there are numerous subcultures that will best be penetrated when churches are run by people from similar ethnic and social backgrounds.

The lack of local leadership is one reason why so many established churches do not grow. These churches do not lack commitment, spiritual depth, or desire. Rather, they have a different cultural makeup as compared to the communities in which they work and serve. For example, a church with a congregation of blue-collar factory workers would most likely have a difficult time making inroads into the ranks of white-collar executives, and vice versa. Though this fact may be disconcerting, it is a reality that church planters must recognize.

During the next few decades, the greatest challenges for church planters will stem not only from increasing ethnic diversity in the country, but also the distinct subcultures that comprise each subsequent generation. Currently, new waves of church planting respond to the needs of more recent generations; this effort must continue to be effectively designed and executed, particularly when churches begin to reach out to the media-savvy Millennial generation.[9]

Socio-Political Factors Affecting Church Planting

Churches are planted to meet the spiritual and often social needs of local communities. The churches are concerned with the morals of the community in which they are located. Churches are particularly helpful in times of need. For example, recently in New Orleans, Louisiana, Hurricane Katrina rendered many people homeless; churches, both inside and outside the area, stepped in to supply food and shelter to those who lost their homes, and jobs were provided to those who lost their belongings to the natural disaster. Churches and the government worked together with the goal of providing and caring for those who are less privileged.

To properly establish a church, numerous decisions must be made, and social, financial, and governmental obligations have to be met. These issues may appear trivial, but they represent an important part of the church planter's job.

Choosing a Name

Choosing a name is very important in church planting. Some church planters have difficulty in choosing a name for the church. Fifty years ago, naming a church was easy because of fewer denominations and greater cultural homogeneity. Now, churches

---

9   Larry L. Lewis, *The Church Planter's Handbook* (Nashville: Broadman, 1992), 12.

adopt unique names that reflect the local community, particularly in urban areas. In some cases, there may be an existing larger church of the same denomination and name, which creates an issue. Some churches may require that a certain title be attached to the name of the church, such as "Assembly," to denote the denomination.

Despite these potential setbacks, a name must still be chosen. The name of a church should reflect its founders' vision for ministry. A church that aims to appeal to a modern fellowship perhaps should not give itself an orthodox name. A church should give itself a name that reflects its purpose.

Registration of the Church

Administrative issues, such as registering the church, cannot be overlooked. There are numerous other organizational tasks that need to be dealt with during this phase. The church planter will be the primary person assuring that these tasks will be completed, but it is helpful if all those involved in the church are aware of what is going on. To this end, organizational meetings should be conducted, whereby the church will be declared as open.

In the initial organizational meeting, the church planting committee will need to elect a temporary chairperson, treasurer, and secretary. The secretary should immediately begin to keep minutes for the fledgling church. These three people, and perhaps one or two others that the group appoints, will comprise the temporary church council. The temporary church council should be charged with organizing the rest of the congregation. The council might also want to appoint a church historian who will be responsible for starting the church archives—arranging for photographs and copies of important documents. During this time, the members of the church council would be well served by spending time in prayer affirming and thanking God for their calling.

Incorporation

The church has to be incorporated. Each state government differs slightly with regard to laws governing incorporation, so each church must check with the secretary of state in the state that will be home to the church. Relevant documents and forms will be filed with the state government.

State Tax-Exempt Status

Most new church plants are affiliated with a mother church. If a church plant is affiliated with another established church, then a tax-exempt letter can be obtained from the mother church. As a result, the new church will be included in the mother church's exemption from government taxes. Once the church is exempted, any contributions made to the Lord's work through the church plant are exempt from federal taxes under section 501(c)(3) of the Internal Revenue Code of 1954.

Taxpayer Identification Number

The church planter must apply for a tax identification number even though the church is exempted from paying federal income tax. This number is called an employer's identification number, or EIN. This is the corporations' equivalent of a Social Security number, and it is issued by the Internal Revenue Service.

Form SS-4, Application for Employer Identification Number, can be obtained from the Internal Revenue Service. Every employee of the church completes this form, which is used to identify the tax exemption for each individual employed by the church.

Mailing Address

A mailing address has to be set up by the church, where all mail to the church will be directed. In case the church is not sure whether it wants to maintain a permanent site, the best option would be to obtain a post office box at a nearby post office.

Telephone Service

The need for a telephone in a new church plant cannot be overemphasized. Sometimes it may appear as if there is no need for a phone, but it will soon be noticed how important a phone can be. It is advisable to choose a phone number that can easily be remembered. The phone number should be set up as a business line so you can be listed in the Yellow Pages. Ensure that the phone is listed in the Yellow Pages under categories that can be easily identified. Information can also be easily accessed through online directories.

Government Regulations

Although the government advocates for the separation of church and state, some government agencies will want to regulate the operations of the church. There are times when their concerns are justified, such as in the case of public safety. Getting zoning permits and passing building inspections can be very political processes in nature and may require government involvement. The church planter should be prepared to entertain the presence of government at all levels and choose how to handle the situations as they arise. When legal matters occur beyond what you can handle, consult a Christian attorney for assistance.

Chapter 1

CHURCH PLANT UNDER REVIEW

Authoritative sources are found on the study of church planting. The most powerful authority in church planting is the Bible. The Bible is the source document handed over to us today that reveals the mind of God to humanity. Christian training and vision are based on what we study and understand from the Bible. Second Timothy 3:16–17 says, "All scripture is given by inspiration of God, and is profitable for doctrine, for reproof, for correction, for instruction in righteousness: That the man of God may be perfect, thoroughly furnished unto all good works."

In line with the purpose of establishing a guiding principle for new church planters, many authoritative sources have been consulted. The relevant literature considered in this study provides practical and theological advice for improving church planting. According to Charles Brock, an effective church planter must be self-governing, self-supporting, and self-propagating.[1] A new church plant must depend on the lordship of Jesus Christ. An indigenous church should garner financial support from its members; eventually, the planted church should be able to begin other new churches.

---

[1] Charles Brock, *The Principles and Practice of Indigenous Church Planting* (Nashville: Broadman Press, 1976), 9.

This chapter will discuss church planting efforts by experienced church planters and an analysis of discoveries made in this area. Literature related to church planting will be discussed accordingly. Information collected from numerous churches, pastors, and laypeople will be collected and assessed. This literature will inform future church planting efforts and will accurately depict the challenges that church planters will face.

Peter Wagner explained in an interview that church planting begins with the pastor. Before planting a church, a pastor must go through a process of self-evaluation, because the quality of ministry is a product of the pastor's personality. If a pastor has stagnated in spiritual, intellectual, or emotional growth, then the ministry is unlikely to be successful. A ministry can only have integrity if it flows from the pastor's identity. Wagner asserted that the most important growth for the church occurs in the senior pastor's heart. Churches are not going to be much better than the people who lead them.

Wagner encouraged the church planter to form a relationship with the community where he or she ministers. Further, he advised that it is important to have individuals in our lives who are willing to challenge us; we desperately need this to protect us from pride. Pride is one of the most destructive things for the ministry. However, if a minister spends time with the Lord, He will help the ministry address its issues with pride.

He advised church planters to guard against the spirit of technology. Technology is something that can be gradually applied to church planting as church leaders find suitable techniques. The abuse of technology can gradually produce a notion among the ministry that it does not need God. Church planters can use technology to grow huge churches that look good but in reality are very sick. If a church relies on gaudy technology for its success rather than the Holy Spirit, then its efforts are in vain. The only churches that are healthy are those that are built with utter dependence on God.

The History of Church Planting

Paul Scott Wilson investigated the authority of the Word as preached by the early disciples. He noted that it took over thirty years after the death and resurrection of Jesus before proper written documents were made of His activities while still on earth.[2] Despite the fact that they were scattered all over the world, the disciples orally documented the efforts of Jesus. They told their stories of Christ for a variety of reasons, as illustrated in the following table:

Table 3

Reasons for Church Planting
i.   As a witness to the good news of Christ
ii   To win followers of Christ
iii In order that details not be forgotten
iv. Because the stories and sayings of Christ made sense of their continuing experience of Him
v.   To shape their own community lives such that their lives would be witnesses to the truth of Christ
vi. To help settle disputes—for instance, with the followers of John the Baptist

---

2   Paul Scott Wilson, *A Concise History of Preaching* (Nashville: Abingdon, 1992), 21.

The disciples created churches as part of their searching the Scriptures for clues to the meaning of Christ, as a form of oral commentary on the Scriptures, and eventually, as a way of understanding their increasing ostracism from the synagogues. Their preaching centered on the stories and sayings of Jesus. If death had been the end of Jesus, then there would be no history of the influence of Jesus, no reason to get involved with Jesus, no faith in Jesus, and no community of those who believe in Him; further, there would be no church, because Jesus would ultimately have been uninteresting for His contemporaries and His disciples.

Fries stated, "The confirmation of Jesus' claim to be the definitive revealer, Messiah, Son, lies, according to unanimous New Testament witness, in the message and in the faith ordered to it: The Crucified One has been raised from the dead; he is risen from the dead. Therefore the resurrection of Jesus, along with all the meanings associated with it, is also the sign and miracle."[3]

Rahner asserted this notion as well, stating,

> The resurrection of Jesus is the essential miracle in the life of Jesus, in which his real meaning is gathered up in radical unity and makes its appearance for us. The resurrection of Jesus calls to us in a more radical way than the individual miracles in the life of Jesus, since the resurrection has both the highest identity of saving sign and saving reality (more than all other conceivable miracles), and because it calls out to our hope of salvation and resurrection which is given us with transcendental necessity.[4]

---

[3] Heinrich Fries, *Fundamental Theology* (Washington, DC: The Catholic University of America Press, 1996), 37.

[4] Karl Rahner, *Foundations of Christian Faith,* Translated by William V. Dych (New York: Crossroad Publishing Co., 1994), 264.

Historically, the church talked about evangelism, both as the Bible's mission and as the means to that mission. Only recently has the concept of church planting been so popularized that evangelism in its broader sense seems improper. Without the greater goal of church planting, evangelism is often thought of as unnecessary.

Ephesians 4 is a great passage that summarizes the overarching goals that God achieves in and through the church. Although Christ works for individuals, He has corporate goals and means, including salvation. Ephesians 4 speaks clearly as to how and why God has gifted and appointed different people in His kingdom. God builds up His people and shapes them into His called-out ones (literally, the meaning of the church). Salvation can never be separated from sanctification. Baptism in Christ incorporates the baptized into the church as Christ's body. This compels them to identify themselves with the earthly local church, for it is there God has designed to accomplish many of His great goals.

Acts 14:23 says, "And when they had appointed elders for them in every church." When there were enough believers and sufficient time, he would appoint elders over that flock. Paul knew what the church should look like. The purpose was not to have some church building but a group of God's people who were responsible to the elders over them, who in turn served God. Jewish believers with their background in the Scriptures accelerated this process.

Church planting is the process of building up the kingdom of God clearly illustrated and taught in the Scriptures. Rightly understood, it helps us understand all the dynamics necessary in building a church so that it will be strong and protected. The establishment of its own leaders enabled them to say there was not a church there. Acts 20:17 says, "He sent to Ephesus and called the elders of the church." These situations are illustrated over and over. In Paul's instruction to Timothy, we see that Timothy as pastor appointed elders. He was cautioned not to anoint new believers to this position.

The Need for Church Planting

Planting a church is simply obeying Jesus' command before He left for heaven. According to Matthew 28:19, Jesus stated, "Go ye therefore, and teach all nations, baptizing them in the name of the Father, and of the Son, and of the Holy Ghost: Teaching them to observe all things whatsoever I have commanded you: and, lo, I am with you always, even unto the end of the world."

Jesus was a church planter. The Bible offers numerous stories of Jesus bringing sinners to repentance. At the well in Samaria, Jesus had an encounter with a Samaritan woman whose life was changed because the power of the gospel was irresistible. The whole city was converted to Christianity because Jesus shared the Word of God with her. According to John 4:23, Jesus predicted, "But the hour cometh, and now is, when the true worshippers shall worship the Father in spirit and in truth: for the Father seeketh such to worship him."

The act of establishing churches in urban areas is as old as the gospel itself. When people move from rural areas to the city, the church must follow the people. For example, Paul was among those who depended on the city for their livelihood. He supported himself, at least partially, by working in the city, making tents. Paul often reminded his audience that he never intended to defraud or deceive them as he presented the gospel. These early preachers—who were church planters—performed their jobs with extreme diligence in order to show an example to a church planter today that it takes dedication and selfless effort to plant a church successfully.

Meeks examined the flow of the US population from rural to urban areas. He noted that people move to cities because they look for opportunities to improve their lives. His research demonstrated that cities offer more economic opportunities to individuals than rural areas. The church planter must be aware of the circumstances that lead people to the urban environment.

When a church planter understands the people's backgrounds, he or she can devise an effective way to reach out to them.

Reaching out to the community is the basis for planting churches. The church planter gathers his or her group into a formidable force to present the gospel to the sinners. According to Acts 2:41–42, "Then they that gladly received his word were baptized: and the same day there were added unto them about three thousand souls. And they continued steadfastly in the apostles' doctrine and fellowship, and in breaking of bread, and in prayers." Those who believed what Peter said were baptized and added to the church—about three thousand in all. They joined with the other believers and devoted themselves to the apostles' teaching and fellowship, sharing in the Lord's Supper and prayer. The establishment of such groups was seen many times throughout the book of Acts and was a major aspect of the apostolic mission. The apostles, in addition to the performance of miracles, established churches.

Nelson Searcy, in his book *The New Paradigm in Church Planting,* asks a question, "What would it look like if your church started a new church? Or if you felt called to plant a church?" Maybe you have dreamed of planting a church, he states, but the logistics of making it happen seem too daunting. You already have a church—and likely a thriving one at that—so why start another one? Why should you consider becoming a launching church?

The above questions could be addressed from a biblical and evangelical standpoint. Churches birthed out of existing, healthy churches have a significant advantage over church plants started from scratch. As a church planter from an existing church, you have the experience, support, and financial backing of your current staff and congregation. If you lead an outwardly-focused church, you already have to teach the people who understand the importance of reaching out into the community. If your people are growing followers of Jesus, they will likely embrace being part of culture that is focused on starting new churches. They want to be part, on some level, of expanded opportunities to share their faith with other areas of the community.

God's church is meant to multiply. In the early days of church expansion, Paul wrote, "The Lord's hand was with them, and a great number of people believed and turned to the Lord" (Acts 11:21). If God is calling anyone to be a church planter, His hand will be with the person as it was with the Christians in Acts.

The path of least resistance is to keep tending our little corners of the world—to let ourselves become busy with the daily concerns of running our churches. But God has called us to spread the gospel more effectively by multiplying. He has called us to touch more unchurched people by taking the truth closer to them. By learning how to biblically and strategically launch new churches, we can grow healthy communities and lead more people to become fully developing followers of Jesus.

The most important factor in the decision to launch a new church is God's leading. You must know that you know you are called. Thriving churches have always been and will always be built on the foundation of personal calling, not personal choice. Once you are certain your call to start another church is from God, start exploring the details. As Guy Kawasaki writes in *The Art of the Start,* "The hardest thing about getting started is getting started."

When you know God has called you to start a church, you will be able to factor those first difficult years with confidence and grace. While there will be periods of trial and uncertainty, knowing you have been called to the work you are doing will keep you moving forward. Look at some ways you can recognize a proper calling:

Prayer and Bible study. God calls and confirms His call through prayer and Bible study. When God calls people, He often confirms His calling every time they pray or read the Bible.

Ministry may have never entered into your own plans when God intercepted them. Someone said, "When God is stirring in my life, everything familiar gets uncomfortable." This surprise calling leads to a 180-degree turn in career and focus.

Holy discontent. While anger, resentment, or discontent toward an existing church or pastor can be sources of improper calling, a proper calling will often carry with it a sense of *holy* discontent. This discontent does not focus on problems within a ministry but has a heart to improve the situation in a particular community. Holy discontent also comes when you have ignored God's call in your life and you realize you will not find fulfillment until you surrender to His will to start a church.

Burden for the unchurched. A desire to reach the unchurched always accompanies a proper call. If your goal is to change the Christians in your community, most assuredly, God has not called you to start a new church. However, if you have a strong passion to reach the unchurched, you may be hearing from God.

Godly counsel. A proper call will be accompanied by the confirmation of those around you. Seek other leaders, and gauge their response to your call.

The Impact of Culture in Church Planting

Planting a church in a diverse culture calls for a dedicated and devoted person who is convinced, without a shadow of a doubt, that God is the one who called. Jesus Christ understood that the world is defined by diverse cultures. When Jesus asked His disciples to preach the gospel to people in Jerusalem, Judea, Samaria, and the utmost parts of the world, He knew that they would encounter numerous difficulties in the process, such as language barriers and incompatibility with other religions and cultures.

As discussed earlier in this study, people from countless different backgrounds and cultures comprise the modern American city. Mainstream American society has struggled with how to cope with this emerging culture. Protestants struggled during the early twentieth century over how to relate to the changing culture. Members of various denominations wondered what happened if one belonged to a long-established Protestant church, such as a Methodist, Presbyterian, or Congregationalist church. Some were confronted with the issue of how Christians should relate to an increasingly pluralistic and secular society. For members of the leadership in such groups, one practical question was whether they could continue to dominate American life. If so, could they retain their traditional Protestant beliefs? Or would they have to modify and broaden those beliefs both in order to remain current with prevailing opinion and continue their cultural influence?

In his book, *Religion and American Culture*, George M. Marsden stated, "Traditional Protestantism, like almost all other Judeo-Christian religions, is exclusivist."[5] Exclusivism teaches that some people will be saved for eternal life, and some will not. Mardsen stated that this type of belief promotes the dominance of one particular viewpoint in society, which brings about misunderstandings in worship.

By the early twentieth century, the United States started embracing the reality of a pluralistic society. It was not known whether the exclusivists were prepared to accept inclusivist teachings; for instance, in order to retain its cultural legitimacy, some Protestants argued that the church should teach that Christianity is just one of the ways by which humans can find God. This type of broadened belief was encouraged by the intellectual outlook of the time that challenged any claims to absolute truth and explained differences in belief systems as a function of differing historical circumstances. There has been a shift in the culture since the nineteenth-century America.

---

[5] George M. Marsden, *Religion and American Culture* (Independence, Kentucky: Cengage Learning, 2000), 168.

Protestantism has been close to the center of power in the United States; it has held its power, because it has kept pace with the cultural change. According to Marsden, "This impulse was a major component in theological liberalism or modernism which believed that Christianity should keep up with and provide leadership for modern cultural and intellectual change by reinterpreting its traditions to fit with modern ideals."[6]

Conservative Protestants and revivalists often strongly dissent with this analysis of the perceived cultural crisis. They note that America's contemporary moral decadence is a problem, emphasizing that America was built and founded on the Bible. Liberal Protestants and secularists, in contrast, attacked the authenticity of the Bible, offering evolutionary-based philosophies as an alternative. The introduction of this worldview led many people, such as William Jennings Bryan, to begin to advocate that humans were nothing more than higher-order animals. Bryan was influenced by a study done in 1916 by James H. Leuba that indicated that over half of American biologists believed neither in God nor immorality. Over time, however, Bryan and a few other scientists began to see things differently. As Bryan put it, "It is better to trust the Rock of Ages ... than to know the ages of the rocks."[7]

In America, the world is changing. Fortunately, Christianity has the adaptive ability to connect with an enormous diversity of cultures around the world. At its worst, Christianity has the lamentable propensity to become fully intertwined with its host culture. When this happens, it is difficult to distinguish where the culture stops and the church begins. Admittedly, it is imperative that Christians communicate and live out the gospel in order to connect people to the message; however, at the same time, the church, by its nature, must be countercultural. The message of Jesus challenges all social, religious, and political powers. The

---

[6] Ibid., 178.
[7] Ibid., 181.

church must navigate between these two polarities. If the church's message is too aggressively countercultural, then few people will hear its words. If the church over-identifies with the culture, the gospel becomes tame and loses its power to transform lives.[8]

Church Growth

A church should be able to generate another church. Jesus intended that the church would grow from Jerusalem to Judea, Samaria, and all parts of the world. For the church to expand, this growth principle must be followed today. Some churches are satisfied with where they are; some are content with their growth or the number of the membership in their churches. It is impressive to see many churches grow from less than two hundred in number to an astronomical number, such as twenty thousand, in a number of years.

Growth of the new church begins the first day after the launch. Growth requires building a relationship list, developing an immediate follow-up process, designing an assimilation plan and a small group development strategy, and working toward legal recognition of the congregation.[9] A new church develops a list of new attendees whenever someone new comes to the church. The church begins to plan strategies to reach out to the community through the list. Individuals who attend church events generally come back to worship or make the new church plant their church home. Stetzer stated that the best way to involve new members is to encourage them to share their names and other pertinent information to the degree that they are comfortable.

---

[8]   David T. Olson, *The American Church in Crisis* (Grand Rapids: Zondervan, 2008), 162.

[9]   Ed Stetzer, *Planting New Churches in a Postmodern Age* (Nashville: Broadman Press, 2003), 300.

The Church Planting Process

Planting a church is a process. It takes a lot of planning before a church is planted. The pastor planting a church must be very visionary. He knows what he wants and goes out of his way to implement what God has deposited in his heart. The pastor is bombarded with countless ideas and wants to ensure that he plants a church that stands the test of time. According to Murray, church planting has taken place for nearly twenty centuries. Church planting is one component in a much broader mission agenda that includes evangelism, discipleship, social action, cultural engagement, political involvement, environmental concern, and much more.[10] Church planting has been of crucial importance throughout history.

The ministry of church planting begins with evangelism. We must speak about the kingdom in our evangelism, because post-Christians are more concerned with the kingdom in this life than with the kingdom in the next life.[11] Evangelism has taken different forms in today's society. In order to reach the modern generation, evangelism has employed the tools of television commercials, radio broadcasting, newspaper advertisements, websites, podcasting, and word-of-mouth.

Once the people are reached, churches have established follow-up protocol, where individual church members are assigned to call visitors and even send them thank you cards or tracts. Some churches organize barbeque sessions and picnics for new and old members of the congregation to ensure sustenance and rekindling of interest among the church attendees. Musical presentations are planned, whereby invitations are sent out to the public to come for gospel jamborees. Many people attend these occasions, and the gospel is preached to them.

---

[10] Stuart Murray, *Church Planting: Laying Foundations* (Harrisonburg, Virginia: Herald Press, 2001), 87.
[11] Dan Kimball, *The Emerging Church* (Grand Rapids: Zondervan, 2003), 283.

The need for Christianity in urban areas cannot be overestimated. Most educated people are located in the urban and suburban areas of the United States. Further, immigrants from other countries generally make their homes in urban and suburban areas as well. People in these areas must find Christ as their personal Savior and Lord in the process of trying to make a living. Suburbia is a place of spiritual impulses and longing—the desire for security, a place to call home, a healthy community, meaningful relationships, and purposeful living. The suburban Christian community also seeks to help others realize the fulfillment of these longings, ushering them into the blessings of the kingdom of God.[12]

The church planter has the responsibility of taking care of the community where God has placed him or her, in both spiritual and developmental terms. In other words, the planter is part of the community where he or she locates his or her church. The church planter must recognize that God has called him or her to do whatever he or she can so that others may experience the fullness of God's peace and life as God intended it to be. If this is done diligently, the church planter may find that God will enlarge the hearts of not only the immediate neighbors, but also that the ripple effect will affect the global mission and increase attendance at church services. Table 1 shows that while attendance at Evangelical churches is generally higher than that of the Catholic or Mainline churches, it can definitely be increased.

---

[12] Albert Y. Hsu, *The Suburban Christian* (Downers Grove, Illinois: InterVarsity Press, 2006), 198.

Table 4

Attendance at Christian Churches in the United States on Any Given Weekend in 2005, by Denomination			
Denomination			
Evangelical	Mainline	Catholic	Total
9.1%	3.0%	5.3%	17.5%

Table 4 indicates that Evangelical attendance outpaces Mainline attendance on any given weekend at a rate of three to one and outpaces Catholic attendance by a rate of about two to one. Those focusing on church planting efforts must take such statistics into account when attempting to maximize their efforts to produce statistically verifiable results. As indicated in Table 5, Murrow comments that men do not go to church, because the left set represents values of Mars, while the right set includes the values of Venus. What is clear from this exercise is that when most people think of Christ and His followers, they think of feminine values. People think of Jesus as having the values that come naturally to women. Thus, true disciples of Jesus should adopt values that are commonly found in women while rejecting those most often found in men.

Table 5

Why Men Don't Go to Church	
Left Set	Right Set
Competence	Love
Efficiency	Beauty
Achievement	Relationships
Skills	Support
Proving Oneself	Help
Results	Nurturing
Accomplishment	Feelings
Objects	Sharing
Technology	Relating
Goal-Oriented	Harmony
Self-Sufficiency	Community
Success-Loving	Cooperation
Competition	Personal Expression

Chapter 2

BIBLICAL AND THEOLOGICAL APPROACH

The Bible states that without vision, the people perish. To carry out God's mandate requires church planters with vision and training in the word of God. The Assemblies of God has established many theological seminaries to train pastors and ministers at all levels. There is no question that the United States of America has become the melting pot of the world. People of diverse cultures, languages, ethnic groups, and professions make up a large population of the country. The need for proper training for church planters cannot be over-emphasized.

Establishment of churches by church planters is a concerted effort that requires a biblical and theological approach. This chapter will discuss the origins of church planting and the effect of early church planting on today's evangelical landscape. The chapter begins with a brief history of how the church was formed and continues with a discussion of the importance of church planting in perpetuating the church's mission. The Assemblies of God has adopted many strategies to reach the United States population with the Word of God.

The Formation of the Church

The formation of what we know today as the church began after the death of Jesus Christ. The religion was first called Christianity in

Antioch during the period of time when the early disciples exhibited an attitude that exemplified the life and character of Christ. In the ancient Roman Empire, pagan society had little concern for the victims of violence and injustice. It was not hard for the Jewish people to categorize Paul as an agent of Mercury and Jupiter when Paul was bitten by a poisonous viper in the island of Melita and he did not die. There was no reason why Zeus or Jupiter should feel sorry for slaves or other victims of misfortune. According to Acts 28:2–4,

> And the barbarous people showed us no little kindness: for they kindled a fire and received us every one, because of the present rain, and because of the cold. And when Paul had gathered a bundle of sticks, and laid them on the fire, there came a viper out of the heat, and fastened on his hand. And when the barbarians saw the venomous beast hand on his hand, they said among themselves, No doubt this man is a murderer, whom, though he hath escaped the sea, yet vengeance suffereth not to live.

Christianity talks about God, who cares deeply about His people. The gospel of Jesus Christ speaks about feeding the hungry, clothing the naked, visiting the sick and imprisoned, and treating strangers kindly (Matthew 25:34–40). Most of these teachings had roots in Judaism, from which Christianity emerged. The Hebrew prophets preached justice for the poor and oppressed as well showing compassion for the impoverished, sick, aged, and enslaved. To love God and to be Christ-like was to love one's neighbor as well as the unlovely and unlovable. To be good meant to be benevolent. Charity became a basic virtue.[1]

---

[1]   Peter Brown, *The Cult of the Saints: Its Rise and Function in Latin Christianity* (Chicago: University of Chicago Press, 1982), 46.

Christians were the first ones to organize early public hospitals, asylums for lepers, and refugee camps for strangers. Christian organizations provided help for widows, orphans, and the sick and disabled as well as relief for the poor. The practice of paganism in Rome called for gift-giving as an act of politics, but Christians converted this as an act of mercy. The historian Peter Brown stressed that women took on a "public role, in their own right, in relation to the poor; they gave alms in person, they visited the sick, they founded shrines and poor-houses."[2]

Growing up in most homes provides memories of religion within families—the daily routines and sacred objects, holidays, and familial relationships. Religious socialization begins in the family. Clergy and other religious leaders would certainly feel that something important were missing if sufficient attention were not paid to congregations.[3] Protestants, Catholics, and Jews of all varieties have always insisted that children learn from an early age to be faithful members of a particular congregation. The idea of sending children to religious services is to train them to better understand their creator and worship Him.

The Christian church was first brought to North American shores by European travelers and settlers. Six nations contended for colonial possession in the New World as they established national churches and missions. Representatives of dissenting traditions also came to the western wilderness, seeking a place of refuge where they hoped to be free to follow their distinctive beliefs. The early immigrants were followed by millions of others who introduced further diversities into the religious picture of the continent. Most of the newcomers came willingly, in search of freedom and prosperity, but those from Africa were brought primarily as slaves, many of whom in time became Christians.

---

[2] Ibid.

[3] Robert Wuthnow, *Growing Up Religious Christians and Jews and Their Journeys of Faith* (Boston: Beacon Press, 2000), 69.

Some of the native Indians were also won to the faith, though never in the numbers that missionaries had hoped.[4] In due course, indigenous churches were planted.

The Church and its Effect on Modern Society

The church has a direct effect on society as a whole. The essence of church is to affect the moral fiber of society. In today's culture, attending church is not as popular as it once was. Church attendance is taken for granted, and some people think that church is not for them. Christianity has always made an impact on the lives of the people. In the days of Noah in the book of Genesis, God wanted to clean up the world. According to Genesis 7:1, "Finally, the day came when the Lord said to Noah, 'Go into the boat with all your family, for among all the people of the earth, I consider you alone to be righteous.'" The mission of Noah was to preach to the people for the great day of the Lord. God was looking for anyone who would be part of the contingent He would save. Only one man was found. God used only Noah and his family to replenish the earth.

God also sent John the Baptist as a messenger before the coming of Jesus Christ. John came baptizing the people as he waited to see the Messiah. His preaching brought many to acknowledge the truth. John did not claim to be the Christ, but many came to be baptized for the remission of their sins. This one act of baptism and remission of sins prepared them for a better life and the waiting of the Savior. John 1:23 related, "John replied in the words of Isaiah; I am a voice shouting in the wilderness, Prepare a straight pathway for the Lord's coming."

Recently, I read about a man who has been a member of the occult for over twenty years. He had lived for so long without

---

[4]   Robert T. Handy, *A History of the Churches in the United States and Canada* (New York: Oxford University Press, 1977), 6.

knowing Jesus Christ that his life was marked with fear and unhappiness. He was known for being wicked, coercive, and ruthless, but he submitted his life to Jesus in a crusade camp conducted by a renowned evangelist of our time. This man now confesses Jesus as Lord, and his life has changed for good.

In Houston, Texas, there is a young man who just graduated from college at the age of twenty-one. He confessed to experimenting with drugs in college, living a promiscuous life, and always lying. He gave his life to Christ in the church one day after as the preacher finished preaching. Today, this man lives righteously before God, works with the pastor, and lives a good life.

When society at large begins to experience the saving grace of Jesus through listening to the Word of God, there is no question that it will radically change for the better due to the planting of churches and preaching of the Word of God. Faith comes by hearing the Word of God. Changing society comes in only one way—hearing the Word of God, which is made possible by church planting.

As the church impacts society positively, there will be need for Christian education. Christian education becomes especially important when church leaders attempt to reach young adults in society. Christian education in a newly planted congregation is not nearly as complicated as that in an established church, but it can be just as vital and even more fun. The church planter can be very creative about this—perhaps making classrooms out of nooks in a movie theater and desks out of clipboards.

To serve young couples, a church planter should make sure that the church plant offers a clean and secure nursery area, preferably with a permanent attendant. Because church planters should try to stretch every dollar, they might be tempted to dispense with established curriculums. However, unless the church employs some very creative and energetic teachers, established curriculums should not be discarded. It is not worth the time and energy to write a new curriculum while trying to get a new church up and running. A church planter might be able to adapt some Vacation Bible School curriculums for use in children's ministries.[5]

The Plan of Salvation

According to Genesis 3:21, "And the Lord God made clothing from animal skins for Adam and his wife." The plan of salvation started as far back as the garden of Eden. When Adam and his wife sinned in the garden, it touched the heart of God. God could not stand sin. Blood had to be shed for the atonement of sin. God wanted immediately to redeem people from their sins. According to Isaiah 53:7–12,

> He was oppressed and treated harshly, yet he never said a word. He was led as a lamb to the slaughter. And as a sheep is silent before the shearers, he did not open his mouth. From prison and trial they led him away to his death. But who among the people realized that he was dying for their sins—that he was suffering their punishment? He had done no wrong, and he never deceived anyone. But he was buried like a criminal; he was put in a rich man's grave. But it was the Lord's good plan to crush him and fill him with grief. Yet when his life is made an offering for sin, he will have a multitude of children, many heirs. He will enjoy a long life, and the Lord's plan will prosper in his hands. When he sees all that is accomplished by his anguish, he will be satisfied. And because of what he has experienced, my righteous servant will make it possible for many to be counted righteous, for he will bear all their sins. I will

---

5   Carl F. George, *Prepare Your Church for the Future* (Tarrytown, New York: Fleming H. Revell Co., 1991), 80.

give him the honors of one who is mighty and great,
because he exposed himself to death. He was counted
among those who were sinners. He bore the sins of
many and interceded for sinners.

God decided that He must make provisions for humanity to
come back to its Creator. Originally, the plan was only for the
Jews, but the grace of God eventually extended to the Gentiles.
The Bible reveals that God accepts anyone who comes to Him,
because Jesus came to reconcile man to God.

Due to sin, humans lost their peace and relationship with God.
God had to send His only begotten Son to save humankind. This is
good news for human beings, because God cares enough to send
His only Son to come to the world to redeem people. The good
news, moreover, is true whether you believe it or not. Too often,
Christians have spoken as if God's love were available only to those
who respond to it in the right way—by believing the doctrines
of a particular creed or confession, following particular rules of
life (the more repressive, the better), having a particular kind of
conversion experience, being born again, belonging to the right
denomination (taken by its members to be the only true church)
or to some group of especially pious people, or reading the Bible
in a certain way and drawing only the right conclusions from it.[6]

The plan of salvation will not be accomplished on
earth without church planting efforts. Peter made
the first sermon on the day of Pentecost, and three
thousand souls came to Jesus. According to Acts 2:14–
16, "Then Peter stepped forward with the eleven other
apostles and shouted to the crowd, 'listen carefully, all

---

[6] L. William Countryman, *Good News of Jesus* (Boston: Trinity Press
International, 1993), 6.

of you. Fellow Jews and residents of Jerusalem! Make no mistake about this. Some of you are saying these people are drunk. It isn't true! It's much too early for that. People don't get drunk by nine o'clock in the morning. No, what you see this morning was predicted centuries ago by the prophet Joel.'"

Acts 2:40–41 continues, "Then Peter continued preaching for a long time, strongly urging all his listeners, 'Save yourselves from this generation that has gone astray!' Those who believed what Peter said were baptized and added to the church—about three thousand in all."

Jesus concluded the work of salvation when He went to the cross and died. He was crucified for the sins of the whole world. The Bible asserts that the salvation plan is made open for anyone who is willing to live righteously for God. The gospel is preached to every creature, because the Son of Man will not come until the gospel has been preached to every creature. God has been very gracious to man. Romans 3:23 reveals, "For all have sinned and come short of the glory of God." Romans 6:23 echoes this theme: "For the wages of sin is death; but the gift of God is eternal life through Jesus Christ our Lord." Romans 10:9 asserts, "That if thou shalt confess with thy mouth the Lord Jesus, and shalt believe in thine heart that God hath raised Him from the dead, thou shalt be saved." It is God's plan to save as many as would trust in Him.

Chaplaincy

The Chaplaincy Department was officially established in 1973. The director is amenable to and serves under the executive director of Assemblies of God US Mission in supervising the work of the department. As the action officer for the Commission of Chaplains, the director is also amenable to the general superintendent, who serves as a chairman of the Commission, which is the Endorsing Agency for the Assemblies of God chaplaincy. The director is appointed by the Executive Presbytery.

The Chaplaincy Department is a model for other denominations to emulate. Based on increasing demand for specially qualified ministries, we envision Assemblies of God chaplains taking leadership roles in federal, state, and other public institutions and organizations because of their highly effective ministry. Chaplains and staff personnel take their divine calling and commitment seriously, combining current communication technology and skills with a keen sense of mission. We seek qualified applicants who will meet high educational and training standards required in ministering to personnel in pluralistic, specialized settings not normally accessible to other clergy.

Our mission is to provide an effective organization to recruit, train, endorse, equip, and supply professionally and academically qualified persons to serve as chaplains in federal, state, and other facilities; provide ancillary guidance and nurture for chaplains who serve in a wide variety of institutional and occupational settings, such as military, veterans affairs, correctional, health care, industry, and other areas; and provide for their support and accountability to US Missions and the Commission on Chaplains.

The primary function of this department shall be to recruit qualified pastors to fill openings in chaplaincy ministry; deliver effective training, including legal issues, at annual chaplains' conferences; provide current information to keep chaplains abreast of changes within their specific areas of ministry; encourage chaplains toward continuing education goals; promote membership and involvement in professional associations; increase the awareness of the denomination at large concerning the viable ministries of our chaplains; provide resources and training for churches and districts; and facilitate the appointment of nationally appointed US missionaries.

Nationally Appointed US Missionaries for Chaplaincy

The majority of our endorsed chaplains do not require US Missions appointment, as they are hired by the government, institutions, or other organizations to fill the role of chaplain. US Missionary appointment then is focused on, but not limited to, facilitating the ministries of chaplain in the more nontraditional areas that have no hiring bodies, such motorcycle clubs, racetracks, rodeo, etc. Chaplain US missionaries must meet the same professional requirements as other endorsed chaplains. They must demonstrate a call to the ministry for which they request appointments to be ordained and have two years of pastoral ministry. US missionary appointment is also available to chaplains serving in more traditional areas of ministry, and support from an outside source must be raised in order to continue the ministry.

Chi Alpha Campus Ministries, USA

Chi Alpha Campus Ministries, USA is the national office working in cooperation with and at the invitation of various districts. The supervision and administration of the work of the missionaries and ministries who have official recognition through national US Missions appointment with Chi Alpha Campus Ministries, USA, are committed to the districts where they are located. Most districts have Chi Alpha Committees led by the district mission's director or a designee. The Assemblies of God has established the national Chi Alpha Campus Ministries Department, USA to provide ministry among the college and university population of the United States, including international students studying on America's campuses.

The college and university campus is a community, sometimes a metropolis, onto itself and is comprised of students, faculty, staff, and leaders-in-training from most nations and religions of the world. The university campus is clearly a distinct culture.

Chi Alpha Campus Ministries, USA exists to serve as an agency of the Assemblies of God for the evangelization and discipling of college and university students, primarily on secular campuses in the United States, and by being a missionary appointing and sending agency as well as facilitating and resource agency for church and campus ministries in reaching collegians. Our vision is to reconcile students to Christ and transform the university students, marketplace, and world. Our mission is the fulfillment of Christ's Great Commission on campus, primarily through the information of ministries on campus.

Chi Alpha Campus Ministries, USA also provides a supplement to the *Assemblies of God US Missions Manual*. In addition to all requirements of a nationally appointed US missionary outlined in this manual, Chi Alpha Campus missionaries are required to sign the itinerating covenant, affiliate annually as campus ministry personnel, and affirm and agree to the Chi Alpha Statements.

Chi Alpha Campus Ministries, USA fulfills its role to college and university students through the following means: provide for the recruitment, appointment, and placement of US (campus) missionaries; provide information, resource, and promotion assistance to district local churches and campus ministries; provide training for staff and students; supervise the work of national representatives who assist in specific areas of the national ministry; and devise strategies and programs for implementing campus ministries. Chi Alpha Campus ministries, USA is committed to evangelism and discipleship of American and international college and university students. The terms *campus missionary, campus director, campus staff, campus minister, campus worker, chaplain,* and *campus pastor* are often used interchangeably and mean the same thing. Generally, this term applies to paid vocational campus workers serving on a college or university campus.

Campus ministry includes personnel who have no ministerial credentials (Campus Missionary Associate), the certified minister (Campus Missionary Appointed Certified), and those who are licensed or ordained (Campus Missionary). Campus Missionary Associates are requested and approved by a local campus missionary or campus director.

With district approval, a certified, licensed, or ordained minister may serve as a campus minister or missionary. The category of campus missionary intern is an approved intern participating in a nationally recognized program. Interns are not staff. They are campus missionary interns.

To qualify as an approved Chi Alpha campus missionary, individuals must attend one annual Reach the University Institute, participate in one nine- to ten-month Campus Missionary Intern program, and pursue ministerial credentials.

Approval by the District

Additionally, to be nationally appointed, the individual must make application for campus missionary service, be invited and interviewed by Chi Alpha Missionary Screening Committee, be approved, and itinerate and raise a full budget.

Campus ministers and missionaries will promote Pentecostal worship; build community on campus; disciple, model, train, and conduct evangelism; pray; develop and train student leaders; teach; counsel; represent Assemblies of God to students and students to the Assemblies of God; network with other campus ministries and ministers; itinerate, raise, and manage budgets; communicate with donors; create and advertise special ministry events; develop personally; educate and provide mission opportunities; facilitate ministry to internationals; and participate in district and national Chi Alpha events.

Church Development

The Church Development Department has been established by the General Presbytery at the initiative of the Executive Presbytery. There will be a department director who will be amenable to and serve under the executive director of Assemblies of God US Missions in supervising the work of the department. He or she will be appointed by the Executive Presbytery. The vision of the Church Development Department is to see the Assemblies of God here at home become a church planting and church multiplication movement. Our mission is to facilitate the Assemblies of God and its constituents in planting a greater quantity and greater quality of healthy, reproducing, kingdom churches.

The Church Development department shall facilitate the planting of churches in the United States in urban, suburban, rural, and recognized special language districts, such as those in which the primary languages are Spanish, Korean, and others; sound the call and vision for church development; offer a proven church planting plan and strategy; and provide effective, biblically sound training for church planters.[7]

The Church Development department must also facilitate the revitalization of growing and declining churches to become reproducing churches, provide networking resources, facilitate the appointment of nationally appointed US missionaries, and provide leadership and training for nationally appointed church development missionaries.

[7] Note Meyer 1953, 103, writer's emphasis

Nationally Appointed US Missionaries
for Church Development

US missionary appointment is focused on facilitating church planting, revitalizing churches, and providing related ministries. Church Development also provides a supplement to the Assemblies of God Missions. US missionary appointment is primarily for those individuals who have a unique church planting call and necessary qualifications to plant a healthy church, bring it to self-sufficiency, and then move on to repeat the process in another location.

US missionary appointment is also available to those who lead ministries that facilitate, equip, encourage, or oversee ministries related to church planting and revitalization.

Intercultural Ministries

The Intercultural Ministries Department is a facilitating agency that works in cooperation with and at the invitation of the various districts. The supervision and administration of the work of the ministers and ministries who have official recognition through the Intercultural Ministries Department are committed to the districts where they are located. The Assemblies of God has established the Intercultural Ministries Department to provide ministry among those groups of people in the United States whose evangelization involves specialized understanding and preparation. These groups are those that have cultural, ethnic, or language distinctiveness; constituting specialized communication groups, such as the deaf and blind; and otherwise forming distinguishable groups.

The Intercultural Ministries Department exists to serve as an agency of the Assemblies of God for the evangelization and discipling of culturally distinct groups in America by being a missionary sending agency as well as a facilitating and resource agency for existing churches in reaching out to the cultural groups throughout the United States of America. The vision is to see the Assemblies of God USA become a fully integrated, culturally diverse fellowship that follows the pattern of the early church in the book of Acts. This would allow cultural groups to remain diverse and distinct while maintaining the unity of the Spirit in the bond of peace.

The Intercultural Ministries Department fulfills its role to these specialized groups through the following means. It provides for the appointment of national US missionaries.

The department serves as liaison to the various ethnic and language groups of the Assemblies of God. Intercultural Ministries also provides a supplement to the Assemblies of God US Missions Manual. The department provides information, expertise, and promotional assistance to districts and local churches. It supervises the work of national representatives who assist in coordinating the work of specific areas of ministry.

The department devises strategies and programs for the development of indigenous leadership among the various groups. The Intercultural Ministries Department is concerned with outreach to America's lost through the following primary areas.

Summer Volunteer

Numerous opportunities are available for youth, college student, and older individuals and couples to share their skills for work and ministry alongside US missionaries, pastors, and directors of various ministries in need of helpers for one- to eight-week missions assignments. College interns find valuable firsthand experience, as do individuals and teams that serve mostly in areas of minor cleanup or repair work to full-fledged camps or community evangelism outreaches involving puppets, mime, drama, music, preaching, and witnessing talents. Summer volunteers are permitted to raise travel and living support from churches where they have family or friends so they can give full-time to their volunteer activities.

One- to Two-Year Missionary Associates

Singles, couples, widowers, and retirees eighteen and older find fulfilling times of service as short-term volunteers in a wide variety of MAPS openings. Whatever one's skills, talents, or interests, most likely, there is a place of service for teachers, accountants, office workers, house parents, cooks, librarians, mechanics, maintenance personnel, musicians, ministry workers, and others at sites throughout America. These MAPS volunteers can have a missions account and are permitted to raise support from churches where they have family or friends so they can give full-time to their volunteer activities.

RV Volunteers

More than 1,400 RV volunteers, most of whom are retired, spend a few weeks to nearly full-time working on MAPS projects as they travel to different places in their motor homes, trailers, and campers. Many use their construction abilities, whether they are skilled or qualify as helpers, building or repairing churches, Teen Challenge centers, children's homes, campgrounds, intercultural sites, and college facilities all across the country. Others use skills as accountants, office workers, librarians, seamstresses, painters, church workers, leaders of Bible studies, and pulpit fill-in and fulfill various evangelism and ministry challenges.

RVers may work alone or in teams with others as they travel from project to project. They pay their own food and travel expenses, but project hosts are responsible to provide water, sewer, and electrical hookups while RVers are on assignments. MAPS office personnel provide information where volunteers are most needed for their prayerful consideration.

MAPS Construction and Evangelism Teams

More than fifty building projects are in need of teams of men and women, both skilled and helpers, to build new churches or repair older facilities. Evangelism activities may be combined with construction work or conducted separately in the form of children's or adult crusades and a variety of witnessing and evangelism outreaches.

Teams consist of two or more people. Often, team members use a week of vacation and pay their own travel, lodging, and meal expenses to serve as volunteers. One church or several congregations may form teams together. Some teams contribute extra funds to help US missions projects purchase needed building materials. Project hosts must have materials on site so MAPS teams can accomplish the most during their stay.

Teen Challenge International, USA

Dave Wilkerson began Teen Challenge in 1958 as an outreach to help members of street gangs build new lives through finding Jesus Christ. As the scope of the drug problem grew, Teen Challenge ministries were started around the country and across the world. There are over two hundred Teen Challenge centers in the United States with a total of approximately six hundred beds for those needing residential care.

The organization of Teen Challenge is similar to that of Assemblies of God churches in that the centers are sovereign, with their own local boards of directors and constitutions. Each center is required to abide by the accreditation standards of Teen

Challenge International and is subject to periodic inspections to verify compliance but is itself governing and responsible for all organizational, personnel, and management decisions. Teen Challenge International, USA's mission is to provide youth, adults, and families with an effective and comprehensive Christian faith-based solution to life- controlling drug and alcohol problems in order to become productive members of society. By applying biblical principles, Teen Challenge endeavors to help people become mentally sound, emotionally balanced, socially adjusted, physically well, and spiritually alive.

The goal of Teen Challenge is to provide prevention programs to the youth of America and take the faith-based proven treatment techniques developed over the last fifty years to the thousands of people who are addicted to drugs and alcohol and see no hope of an effective solution.

Table 7

Ten Challenge International, USA, Exists To:
i   Provide curriculum and resources both to our centers as well as to those who have similar ministry goals for the propagation of the gospel.
ii   Provide certification, certification standards, and policies for Teen Challenge International, USA. Act as a conduit for Teen Challenge Centers to communities across the country, churches, the Assemblies of God headquarters, and other ministries within the Assemblies of God.
iii   Teen Challenge centers on a national level to media, government entities, and other organization of national scope.

iv Provide for the appointment of national US missionaries in the Teen Challenge organization.
iv Provide leadership to the Teen Challenge organization on a national level. Teen Challenge International, USA also provides a supplement to the *Assemblies of God US Missions Manual.*

Nationally Appointed US Missionaries for Teen Challenge

US missionary appointment is focused on facilitating the operation of the local Teen Challenge facility, providing for ministry to those caught in addictions.

US missionary appointment is primarily for those individuals who have a unique call to minister and have demonstrated the necessary qualifications to provide leadership in a Teen Challenge setting.

US missionary appointment is also available to those who lead ministries that facilitate, equip, encourage, or oversee ministries within the structure of Teen Challenge International, USA.

US missionary appointment is available to Teen Challenge executive directors and immediate support staff based on the recommendation of their Assemblies of God district office.

Youth Alive

Youth Alive (YA), a ministry of the National Youth Ministries of the Assemblies of God, functions under the umbrella of the Assemblies of God. US Missions is a facilitating agency working in cooperation with and at the invitation of the various districts. All nationally-appointed missionaries shall be amenable to the district leadership in which they minister in cooperation with the policies set forth by Youth Alive and the Assemblies of God US Missions. Youth Alive is a campus ministry strategy to present Jesus Christ, the message of hope, to every student on every campus.

Youth Alive strives to establish and assist ongoing campus ministry for every middle, junior high, and senior high school campus. Youth Alive is committed to providing encouragement, resources, and training for students and leaders.

Youth Alive fulfills its role of providing ministry to the campus community through the following means.

Table 8

Functions of Youth Alive
i   Serve as a liaison to the various secondary campus ministry efforts (middle, junior high, and senior high) within the United States
i   Provide information, resources, support, expertise, and promotional assistance to student leaders, local churches, and districts
iii   Facilitate the work of nationally-appointed Youth Alive directors who assist in coordinating the ministry to the students, leader, churches, and organizations on campus
iv   Devise strategies and programs for the development of an ongoing campus ministry to America's middle, junior high, and senior high schools

Nationally Appointed US Missionaries for Youth Alive

Each Youth Alive director is concerned with the evangelization and discipleship of the students who attend America's middle, junior high, and senior high schools. The objective of the nationally-appointed missionary is to promote the Youth Alive goal of reaching every student with the gospel of Jesus Christ before he or she graduates high school.

Recent US laws that have opened doors for ministry on campus refer merely to the students themselves—not to outside adults. Realizing this, nationally-appointed Youth Alive directors realize their goal is to mobilize and equip students and leaders to reach their schools for Christ.

Chapter 3

REKINDLING THE VISION

Revitalizing church planting in North America is a dream that must be realized. In recent time, science has grown so fast that the church planter must be well acquainted with the new technology in other to be successful in planting churches.

This is the age of scientific innovation. Church is no longer old-fashioned. The church planter must have vision and be trained in areas of computer usage as well as different fields of science. The church planter must grow with the new scientific developments.

Scientific innovation has been the order in today's society. This is the computer age, and development in science and technology has left the Christian world with no option but to adjust itself accordingly. Research and development have resulted in areas that were not relevant in the past but are now very relevant in twenty-first-century society. The church planter has to embrace the emerging society and culture in order to make an impact in the world, as Jesus commanded.

The church does not exist in isolation. Modern society is made up of worshippers and non-worshippers. The church planter is part of society, which means that he or she has to be abreast of his or her environment. There are issues important to modern society that the church planter must study in order to find out how these issues relate to the Scriptures or influence the church.

Four current issues about which the church can speak include euthanasia, stem cell research, abortion, and homosexuality.

Euthanasia is the act of ending someone's life in order to prevent the suffering and agony of death; it is also called mercy killing. In performing a mercy killing, a person may feel that he or she is helping humanity. However, the Bible takes a stand on this matter. Exodus 20:13 states, "Thou shall not kill." Even if it is a mercy killing, it is not the duty of any person to take life under any circumstance. The church planter has the obligation to teach the congregation about the truth of God without fear or favor. Many people oppose assisted suicide because they feel it is immoral and unjust, but others believe that it is a humane thing to do if a patient is terminally ill and suffering.

Over the years, there has been a great deal of controversy about this issue. Currently, thirty-six states have specifically outlawed assisted suicide. One doctor, Jack Kevorkian, was present for more than forty assisted suicides. He believed in allowing people to make their own choices as to whether they wanted to live or die. Dr. Kevorkian called the machine that he used on the victims the Thanatron ("death machine" in Greek).[1]

Stem cell research is another important issue in modern society. Adult stem cells are undifferentiated cells found throughout the body after embryonic development that divide to replenish dying cells and regenerate damaged tissues. Also known as somatic stem cells, they can be found in children as well as adults. The church planter must be aware of the consequence of these scientific innovations as well as the Bible's teachings. Indeed, God had already commissioned humans to use their bodies to promote the continuation of the species. Genesis 9:7 stated, "And ye be fruitful, and multiply; bring forth abundantly in the earth, and multiply therein."

---

[1] Microsoft Encarta Online Encyclopedia 2008. "Jack Kevorkian." http://encarta.msn.com/encyclopedia_761589504/kevorkian.html.

Abortion is the premature termination of pregnancy. Intentional termination of pregnancy is not of God. One school of thought believes that life begins at the point of conception, while another believes that life starts at some point following the creation of an embryo. However, Jeremiah 1:5 states, "Before I formed thee in the belly I knew thee; and before thou camest forth out of the womb I sanctified thee, and I ordained thee a prophet unto the nations."

As the Scripture says, God is the creator of humankind—and everything else. He does not intend or plan that pregnancy be terminated at any time. No human knows the plan of God. No one knows who the Messiah will be, so how can people avoid terminating the pregnancy of the Messiah? Who could imagine what the world would be like if Mary, Hannah, or Sarah had terminated the pregnancy of their respective sons, who changed the whole world? Christians are world-changers.

Homosexuality refers to sexual behavior with or attraction to people of the same sex. As a sexual orientation, homosexuality refers to having sexual and romantic attraction primarily or exclusively to members of one's own sex; it also refers to an individual's sense of personal and social identity based on those attractions, behaviors expressing them, and membership in a community of other who share them.[2] However, the Bible speaks clearly on the issue of homosexuality.

Proverbs 2:14–15 states, "Who rejoice to do evil, and delight in the forward of the wicked; whose ways are crooked, and they forward in their paths." Genesis 19:5 states, "And they called unto Lot, and said unto him, Where are the men which came in to thee this night? Bring them out unto us, that we may know them." Genesis 19:27 states, "And Abraham got up early in the morning to the place where he stood before the Lord; And he looked toward Sodom and Gomorrah, and toward all the land of the plain, and

---

[2] APA Help Center website, 2004. "Sexual Orientation and Sexuality," http://www.apahelpcenter.org/articles/article.php?id=31.

beheld, and, lo, the smoke of the country went up as the smoke of a furnace." If God destroyed Sodom and Gomorrah because of homosexuality, He will do it again. This needs to be present in the mind of the church planter. He or she should address this topic accordingly without mincing words.

The spirit-filled church, as in Joel 2:28–29, states, "And it shall come to pass afterward, that I will pour out my spirit upon all flesh; and your sons and your daughters shall prophesy, your old men shall dream dreams, your young men shall see visions: And also upon the servants and upon the handmaids in those days will I pour out my spirit."

This was a prophecy many years before the day of Pentecost. This prophecy was confirmed after the death and ascension of Jesus Christ. Jesus had promised to send down a comforter who would bring the disciples into all the truth. According to Acts 2:1–4,

> And when the day of Pentecost was fully come, they were all with one accord in one place. And suddenly there came a sound from heaven as of a rushing mighty wind, and it filled all the house where they were sitting. And there appeared unto them cloven tongues like as of fire, and it sat upon each of them. And they were all filled with the Holy Ghost, and began to speak with other tongues, as the Spirit gave them utterance.

The spirit-filled church has a serious impact on its environment. This is apparent from the story of Paul, who was cast into prison. According to Acts 16:25, "And at midnight Paul and Silas prayed, and sang praises unto God: and the prisoners heard them." The power of the Holy Spirit moved the prison yard. An earthquake came down, and the whole prison shook because the Spirit of God was at work.

The power of the Holy Spirit still moves today in the church. The power of God brings about healing in the church and miracles of all sorts that take place in every Christian environment where people serve God in holiness and faith. It changes the outlook of Christianity when the power of God is demonstrated, either in a crusade ground or anywhere the name of the Lord is called. In a spirit-filled church, as the songs go on, Christians speak in tongues, and there is an interpretation as the heavenly language comes down in the form of prophecy. Only those who know and believe the Bible will recognize the power of God in action. Some Christians do not believe in the expression of the power of the Holy Spirit in the church, but it is real and effective.

The Relationship between the Church and the Kingdom of God

The church is the bride of Christ. Therefore, it is important to examine the nature of the church and who comprises it. Jesus said that He will build His church, and the kingdom of hell cannot prevail against it. Again, He said that our bodies are temples of the living God. Jesus said that where two or three are gathered in His name, He is among them. Therefore, the formation of the church begins with a few people who decide to get together for a common purpose—to worship God.

In the past century, denominationalism was a very large part of what it meant to be Christian. People were Baptists or Presbyterians, or another denomination, as much as they were Christians. Their Christian identities were inseparable from these denominational traditions. But denominationalism has, as we know, declined in many ways. Fewer people strongly assert that one denomination has a better grasp on the truth than other denominations, and fewer denominations themselves impose creedal tests that people must meet in order to become members or participate in church services. Growing numbers of churches might be characterized as open systems, attempting to embrace everyone.[3]

The church represents God on earth. When Jesus taught and talked with His disciples before His ascension, He had already made a plan for the church. John 14:1–4 states, "Let not your heart be troubled: ye believe in God, believe also in me. In my Father's house are many mansions: if it were not so, I would have told you, I go to prepare a place for you. And if I go and prepare a place for you, I will come again, and receive you unto myself; that where I am, there ye may be also. And whither I go ye know, and the way ye know."

This statement confirms that He will one day come back to take the church to himself. Acts 1:11 states, "Which also said, ye men of Galilee, why stand ye gazing up into heaven? This same Jesus which is taken up from you into heaven, shall so come in like manner as ye have seen him go into heaven."

There is great relationship between the church and the kingdom of God. According to Revelation 21:2–4,

> And I saw the holy city, new Jerusalem, coming down
> from God out of heaven, prepared as a bride adorned
> for her husband. And I heard a great voice out of
> heaven saying, Behold, the tabernacle of God is with
> men, and he will dwell with them, and they shall be
> his people and God himself shall be with them, and
> be their God. And God shall wipe away all tears from
> their eyes; and there shall be no more death, neither
> sorrow, nor crying, neither shall there be any more
> pain: for the former things are passed away.

The kingdom of God is prepared for the church and is made available to all who will submit their lives to Jesus Christ.

---

[3]   Robert Wuthnow, *Christianity in the 21st Century: Reflections on the Challenges* (New York: Oxford University Press, 1993), 49.

The Coach and the Church Planter

Church planting may appear so spiritual that people do not see reason for a coach. However, for every field of endeavor, best performance is exhibited when one can strategize to get the best out of an individual. Mentorship could be interchangeable with the coaching principle. In order to harness the best talent in a church planter, proper training and instructions are needed from individuals who have the required experience in the same field.

Just like in any sport, the church planter needs a *coach*. A *coach* is someone who serves as a special encourager for a minister or pastor. A church planting coach is generally a person who has already successfully planted a church. A good coach brings out the best in a leader. He or she helps the minister's perspective and tells the minister what leadership actions need to be taken.

Coaching is a respectful process in which a coach brings out the higher vision that already exists in a leader. In some circumstances, coaches may provide advice and guidance in a respectful manner, listening to the beliefs, hopes, dreams, and aspirations of the person he or she coaches. In the end, a coach uses his or her experience to help a leader reach his or her highest leadership potential.[4]

Steve Nicholson, a church planter, discussed his coach:

> His encouragement was real help, as well. There was a
> several-month period—especially when only a handful
> people were coming to our introductory Sunday
> evening services—when I felt utterly depressed.
> Soon after that we were without a worship leader for

---

[4]   Church Coaching Solutions. "Leadership Coaching." http://www.church-coaching.com/article/coaching for church leaders.

a period, and I had real anxiety that we were going to lose momentum. Just hearing from Dan that he thought I was approaching things the right way, that these things were a normal part of church planting, and that he had gone through similar—and worse—experience, helped a lot."[5]

It is important to clarify the necessary steps of building a successful coach-church planter relationship. Just as any coach in any sport contributes to a large extent to winning the game, church planting coaches also strongly support the success of the church planter. The better the coach, the more likely the church planter will successfully actualize the dream of church planting, even if the aim is planting numerous churches.

The need for a good coach cannot be overstated. The five phases of the coaching relationship are enumerated below.

> *The Buddy Phase.* Most coaching relationships begin at this stage. The coach and the church planter are "buddies." However, the coach and the church planter should not become lax in establishing clear, delineated expectation. Much attention should be given toward mutual expectations during this phase. If things get rough as time goes on, then the coach and the planter can rely on these defined expectations.

> *The Lack of Trust Phase.* This comprises the second phase, in which either the planter or the coach, or both, demonstrates a lack of trust through their

---

[5] Steve Nicholson, *Coaching Church Planters: A Manual for Church Planters and Those Who Coach Them* (Stafford, Texas: Association Of Vineyard Churches USA, 2008), 9.

actions or words. This is a difficult phase to work through, and the sponsoring church leadership must do everything possible to keep this phase from derailing the entire effort.

The Dislike Phase. The severity of the dislike phase often depends on how well things are going. Not many coaching relationships are able to avoid this phase. Coaches should make sure not to exacerbate this phase, always seeking to keep the relationship vital and healthy.

The Determination Phase. During this stage, many partnering churches feel relief because the turbulence has settled down. Progress in the church plant will excite the planter and his coach. Usually, this stage occurs when the church is making significant progress, and success can be anticipated. This phase holds excitement for both the coach and the planter.

The "It was All Worth It" Phase. The sponsoring church and the new work team will eventually move into a phase in which they recognize the struggle was all worth it. The joy of sponsoring a new church stems from transforming a place that was in darkness into light.

Table 9

Ten Reasons to Consider a New Work Coach
i.   To get an outlook from someone who has no vested interest in the situation's conclusion
ii. To help shed light on God's vision
iii. To point out what the leader can't, won't, or doesn't see
iv. To have an empathetic, secure, and private outlet to vent problems and frustrations
v. To conduct reality checks as the vision progresses
vi. To guide in times of conflict
vii. To put into practice the master plan in appropriate progression
viii.To ask the questions that no one else asks
ix. To develop strategies for recruiting, transitioning, and developing funds
x. To help the church planter balance the demands and stress of leading a church while maintaining a healthy family life

Table 10

Desirable Characteristics of Coaches
i   The new work coach must have a deep-seated passion for the church plant and for the individuals who make up the church planting team.
ii   The new work coach must love the planter, and the planter's family, and all members of the new work team. Caring about the church plant alone is not enough; the work coach must care for the individual members of the church planting team also.
iii   The new work coach must have evangelism as a primary tenet and be able to coach the church planting team in evangelism, outreach, and witnessing effectively. Relationship-building is wonderful, but it must lead to evangelism, or else it is just hanging out.
iv   The new work coach should also be a good listener; he or she should learn what is happening in the church planter's life. The ability to listen well and ask effective questions is perhaps the single most important key to good coaching.
v   The new work coach must have some level of experience in planting New Testament churches. A church host should not allow an inexperienced individual to coach its planter.
vi   The new work coach must be able to deliver the medicine without causing the ill to get sicker. Heavy-handed coaching usually creates a huge disconnect with the planter and the new work team. Often, it is not repairable if all the coach does is criticize and scold.

vii The new work coach must be willing to make this coaching partnership a long-term commitment, perhaps as long as three years. Several church planting movements suggest twelve to eighteen months, but experience demonstrates that at the end of eighteen months, the new work is just getting moving.

Church Planting Models

The church planting process may cut across cultural boundaries and dimensions. There are varieties in worship that necessitate different kinds of church planting models. There are churches that come about through natural birth, adoption, and implantation. There also multi-congregational churches that may take the form of a combination of natural birth, adoption, and implantation. Following is an example of each model within the framework of a church started at a physical distance from the sponsor.

Natural Birth

In an example of the natural birth model, a church planter decided to plant an ethnic church in a neighborhood geographically removed from the planting church. Both key laymen and pastoral leaders saw spiritual needs in a specific neighborhood that were not being met. It was impossible to bring the people to the sponsor's neighborhood on a weekly basis for a variety of reasons.

Table 11

Reasons for New Church Birth
i It was physically too far to transport them.
ii The socioeconomic difference would create a barrier.
iii The language would create a wall between the sponsoring church and the ethnic church.

They were able to transfer this burden to others in the church by planting a new church in that area. The neighborhood had some evangelical churches but none of the sponsor's denomination. Two families in the sponsoring church had retained their original language but adopted American culture. So there were numerous challenges that a new church would help to overcome.

The natural birth model produced many beneficial ideas that can be used by other church planters in a similar situation. The people in the congregation and the community rightly believed the money they gave for this project was for missions, so they were generous in their support of the project. They shared their facilities with the baby church for special occasions, and the sponsor was able to loan its building to the new church for a period of time. The sponsoring church was able to offer advice and support to the mission in fundraising.

People from the sponsoring church were also able to offer advice and support to the mission in fundraising. Leaders of the sponsoring church offered their expertise in long-range planning to help plan the church's long-term goals, and ministers offered fellowship to the mission pastor from the very beginning of the project. Finally, the church staff assisted in goals for weaning the mission work from the sponsoring church, both in finance and leadership.

The Adoption Method

When planting a church using the adoption method, the sponsoring church finds an existing church in another neighborhood and adopts it to help in its development. The situation in this example had many of the characteristics that indicate that the adoption method would be a good model for planting a church.

Many from the adopted church were new in the United States and did not understand the American business structure. Some business matters, like building payments, pastoral support, etc., were confusing to them.

When the established church adopted this new church and helped it develop, many benefits came about. The sponsoring pastor did research on the culture of the group and learned a few phrases of greeting in French language. He educated his congregation on the culture of the mission. He taught the members of his church that they were giving to mission in their own city. Using an interpreter, the sponsoring church trained Sunday school workers, musicians, and social workers.

On Thanksgiving, the sponsoring members showed their love by reaching out to the extremely needy in the mission group. The sponsoring church expressed tangible appreciation to the mission pastor at Christmas. Those with financial expertise gave leadership and training on tithing, budgeting, and a detailed program to help the mission be self-sufficient. English was taught using the Bible as a text.

The Implantation Model

Planting a church using the implantation method involves a sponsoring church that begins an targeted mission in its building and realizes eventually that it will need to be transplanted to a neighborhood where it can grow. For the implantation model to work, a church must have the following characteristics.

Table 12

Characteristics of Church Implantation Model
i   The sponsoring church must have adequate space to begin a new work
ii   There must be adequate transportation to bring in the group.
iii The target group generally lives in one geographical neighborhood.
iv   The sponsoring church must agree that when the target group becomes strong, it will be implanted in the existing church.

In the named example, there was an existing church of the same denomination as the target group in the neighborhood, but several problems existed, including the fact that the existing church was too small to accommodate everyone and the pastor had no cross-cultural experience and could not give the needed help to the target group. Additionally, the existing church could not financially, emotionally, or spiritually support the target mission.

Many things made this model much easier to implement in this case. The target church began in a positive, supportive atmosphere, and all three churches involved were informed from the beginning of future plans. The target mission received help from other uninvolved churches as they relocated to the small existing church. As a result of using this method, the pastor of the existing church in the target neighborhood gained many insights into cross-cultural church planting by being involved from the beginning.

Introduction to Multi-Congregational Churches

A recent study conducted by the Church of the Nazarene has resulted in proposed organizational changes to give guidance to several congregations sharing one facility (multi-congregation). In the report following, facts concerning multi-congregation in the denominations were revealed.

From its inception, the Church of the Nazarene has recognized the opportunity to minister to immigrant groups. Dr. Bresee had both Spanish and Chinese language works in the original First Church of the Nazarene in Los Angeles, California. Therefore, the mother church was a multi-congregational church.

Today, the most conservative statistics we have indicate there has been tremendous growth in multi-congregations churches since 1970. The number of US and Canadian multi-congregations churches have grown from one in 1976 to twenty-two in 1980 and 121 in 1984. This is a 600 percent increase from 1981–1984. If this growth continues, it indicates that before 2090, at least 30 percent of our US and Canadian churches will be multi-congregational. Of the 450 ethic works in existence in 1983 (either fully organized churches or church-type missions), nearly 60 percent meet in the multi-congregational church setting.

Such churches are developed because there is an immediate need for them. People who have recently been uprooted from their cultural setting are very receptive to the gospel message. We may be too late if we try to reach many of these groups by traditional means.

When we see the potential for growth among African-Americans, Koreans, Hispanics, Armenians, Filipinos, Chinese, Cambodians, and other ethnic groups, the possibilities for organizing new areas of ministry develop. In words of the founder of the Church of the Nazarene, Dr. Phineas F. Bresee, "We are debtors to give the Gospel to every creature in the same measure that we have received it."

The multi-congregational churches can be planted using the different models described above or by using a combination of those models. Following are some examples of different types of multi-congregational churches and outlines of how the different models can be used to establish them.

More than One Organized Church Meeting in the Same Building

When more than one church meets in the same building, all congregations work in a continuing fellowship to build unity. All expenses associated with the use of the building facilities are shared proportionately by each group. Each group is equally accountable to the district or state church organization. This section reviews three case examples of how multi-congregational churches can come about through the church planting models of natural birth, adoption, and implantation. Each of the cases reveals how the specific distinctions between the church planting styles affected the development of the multi-congregational church. In addition to the information discussed here, please see appendix 1, model number two.

Case 1: Natural Birth

This example involved a church that planned another church within its facilities with the intention of keeping it there. The English-speaking church was located in a multicultural neighborhood. Through a survey, this church found the community to have five major language groups, including English. Most of the people preferred to speak their own language and have major social contact within their own culture. The youth and children spoke the common language, English, as they went to school and social events together. The exception to this group was preschoolers and recent overseas arrivals. The cost of land prohibited the purchase of five different church properties. The mother church had a building that could be converted for multi-use.

In this example, there were many positive results. The pastor of the English-speaking church preached once a month for a year on biblical understanding of culture, race relations, love, and cross-cultural evangelism. This took place before any non-English service started. The planting took place systematically, starting with the largest language group represented in the neighborhood. The financial support was through the mission giving of the church. Each church was pastored by a person from the target ethnic group, and eventually, all buildings and properties became the responsibility of all the organized churches according to their abilities.

An elected council from each church governed the combined projects of the churches. These included building and property needs as well as Sunday school activities. The five churches hired one youth pastor and one children's minister to pastor the combined needs, since both age groups spoke English. Each local church had its own evangelistic thrust, social outreach, and care of its own church family. The council planned combined services and potluck dinners for cultural awareness once a quarter.

Case 2: Adoption

In this example, the church reached out to an existing church in its neighborhood and adopted the church into its church family. They shared facilities but existed as two separate organizations.

This was an English-speaking church with facilities larger than it needed. This congregation was aware it was in a multiracial area. The congregation was approached by another ethnic church in the area that had no place to meet. The doctrinal stand of both churches was similar, and facilities could be shared by adjusting the time schedule.

An agreeable financial arrangement made each church able to exist easier than before. As a result, both churches thrived. A new sense of mission was felt by the adopting church as it shared its facilities. The pastor led his people to the understanding that the church assisted in the evangelizing of the neighborhood that it previously had not been able to reach.

The financial benefits from this arrangement were significant. Because of the generosity of the English-speaking church, the ethnic group developed deep respect for its people as Americans and for their denomination. Picnics, combined services, and informal fellowship brought each congregation to a new understanding of one another. The English church provided a new base for sponsoring immigrants from the ethnic homeland. There were additional educational benefits as well: English as a second language was taught, and youth and children's English classes were shared by both congregations, because they went to school together.

Case 3: Transition

In this example, the neighborhood had changed. A new church was formed to take over the facility as the existing culture died out. Cities grow, evolve, and decline. Sometimes, there will be a rebirth and resurrection. Transition is a relative term, because it can be slight or a complete change. All of the examples in Chapter 4 are examples of churches in transition. But in this case, complete change took place in the community. For the church to continue to exist, it had to have a racial as well as a socioeconomic change.

The neighborhood began racial changes about twelve years ago. It had made a 95 percent change when this transition took place. The church was white, but as black members moved in, whites moved to the suburbs. The church had a small debt, but it was too large for a struggling black church. The maintenance and utilities were enormous. The congregation could not afford a staff. The church was plagued by vandalism, problems of how to feed the poor, and other social problems.

An interim pastor was called who was experienced in a changing neighborhood. White and blacks members attended Sunday afternoon discussions on issues involving the change. Later, a black pastor replaced the interim pastor. He started a service in free gospel style. The traditional service of the past continued as well.

The new congregation promoted uplift and self-esteem. The black members of that neighborhood were told six days per week that they were a minority, but on Sunday, they were made to feel important. The solving of social problems was linked to the evangelistic outreach. The church organized small geographical groups designed to care for each person individually. These care units promoted the idea that everybody cared for them. Because of the interim situation moving so smoothly, no financial help was needed from outside sources.

More than One Culture in One Church Organization

This model includes several congregations in one church organization, or it could include several language classes that meet separately but are all part of one organization. Each group or class in this type of example has its own leader. Where possible, ethnic leadership is desirable. Each group is accountable to the pastor and local church board. Church board committees have the responsibility of developing programs. These groups may or may not become fully organized churches. However, they may come into membership of the sponsoring organized local church. Following are several examples.

Case 1: Multi-Worship Service

In this example, more than one worship service was held in the same facility. The service may have been cultural but was usually language-based. The neighborhood consisted of four distinct racial, cultural, and/or language groups. The mother church wished to reach the neighborhood and its complex needs through the present structure and facilities. The building owned was adequate to meet services in several areas at the same time. Most of the young people and children spoke English. Immigration continued to feed the neighborhood with new people from the four main groups. The unique circumstances of this situation required some creative organization. Each congregation had its own pastor; they were staff members of the whole church. Combined services were held as often as possible to promote unity.

Fiscal organization was also non-standard. Financial responsibilities were established among the congregations. Payments were made not as rent but to help with the church budget. Representatives from each congregation served on the local church board of the governing body.

When organizing Sunday services, the organizers took into account the unique cultural circumstances. All congregations' Sunday schools met at the same time. Youth and children of all congregations met together when possible. Adults had elective classes, including Bible study in their own language and English as a second language. In the ESL class, the Bible was used as a text, and studying English was combined with Bible truth. Each language group had classes during the week to train its laypeople. Literature advertising the church was distributed in all four languages, thereby displaying to the community a spirit of unity in the church.

Case 2: Multi-Language Classes

In this case, many new immigrants moved in who needed to learn in their own language. Bible studies were altered to help meet their needs. Ten different language groups of immigrants and refugees moved into this neighborhood. No other evangelical group worked with these groups, and the sponsoring church had adequate space to have several classes meeting simultaneously. All groups seemed to coexist in the neighborhood with little friction.

There was a strong desire among refugee and immigrants groups to make money in America. Most realized that they had to first learn English to get a good job. English classes were set up, and US government literature was used to understand the various cultures and language characteristics.

The church was altered to accommodate new immigrant arrival by the local ethnic groups. Social services were set up to help with clothing, food, housing, and adjustment to the new country for these newcomers. People graciously used their gifts to teach even when they had little training—this was particularly true among senior citizens. A missionary who had many successful years overseas was recruited to supervise the program. His support came from churches in the area. This church was ready to start worship services in a few of the language groups whose people were receptive to the gospel.

Case 3: Multicultural

This church designed its services for a variety of cultural groups. All cultures spoke a common language, although this was not always their mother tongue. Most of these cultural groups were upward-moving socioeconomically and wished their children to learn and socialize in the language of the church. In this particular case, that language was English. The service tended to be less formal than average. Musical instruments, both stringed and brass, were often used. Each cultural group was encouraged to promote social events and keep the congregation aware of its heritage.

Once again, the church organizers used creativity in accommodating their multicultural congregation. The pastor stayed current on world news that involved the homelands of his new parishioners and used this material in his sermons. Classes were taught to help children born in America to learn their own native language. Public worship services were carefully sprinkled with prayers and songs from the language represented.

The governing board was selected to include as many cultural groups as possible. This was done through careful nomination and not by designation of each group on the ballot. Various cultural holidays and religious observations were recognized and celebrated when appropriate. Dressing in national costumes gave excitement to these special Sundays. Evangelism was encouraged by bringing family and friends to church dinners with emphasis on one particular ethnic food.

More information has been exhibited on appendices I, II, and III. These appendices speak of themselves regarding church models.

Chapter 4

REDISCOVERING CHURCH PLANTING

As new church planters begin to discover their passion for church planting, it is important to set some guidelines to help them actualize their dreams. The specifics of church planting vary from context to context. However, four general guidelines are fundamental in every church planting situation: spirituality, visualization, communication, and relationships.

Church planters must look at their work as a spiritual activity. They must pray and fast both for the city in which God has placed them and for God to empower them to evangelize. Church planters must recognize that the people of their area who have not yet become followers of God are still under the dominion of Satan. Christ, however, has come "to destroy the devil's work" (1 John 3:8). Church planters, therefore, must pray for wisdom and empowerment from God, realizing that evangelization is the act of taking territory that once belonged to Satan and claiming it for the kingdom of God.

Prayer is an admission of God's role—an acknowledgement that only God can deliver people from the grip of sin and the clutches of the evil one. Evangelizing to unbelievers and nurturing them to grow in Christ is not primarily a human endeavor but rather God working through His people.

Church planters must visualize what God's church should look like within their target culture and seek to implement this vision. In every culture, the church must reflect the presence of

God. However, the form of the church will vary from culture to culture. The form of the church can vary by language, type of worship, and decision-making.

There are numerous questions that a church planter must ask as he or she defines a vision for the church. For example, should a Russian church speak English in worship services? Should the songs reflect the rhythms and harmonies of Western music? Are decisions made by foreigners or nationals, by voting or consensus?

Christian messages must be communicated in indigenous forms. The people of the land should not perceive the church as a foreign institution but rather as a part of the indigenous society. This does not mean that Christianity should be compromised by non-Christian religious elements. It means, rather, that Christian beliefs will be communicated in terms acceptable and meaningful to the culture in which the church is planted. Like a banana plant in the Bahamas, the church can thrive in a particular culture because God allows a church plant to thrive on the resources of the culture rather than superficially borrow cultural forms.

Church planters must learn to communicate God's eternal message in culturally specific ways. The thought that Christ has defeated the principalities and powers has little impact on secular Americans who have little understanding of spiritual powers. Only in Christ is there deliverance from the fear and control of the satanic realm. Church-planting missionaries thus enter a new culture as learners; planters must seek to understand how to communicate God's message and initiate a church that reflects the kingdom of God within a particular cultural context.

Finally, the church planters must be aware of the web of relationships that tie people of different cultures together. In many societies, every person associates not only with brothers, sisters, and grandparents, but also with cousins, uncles, aunts, great-uncles, sisters-in-law, mothers-in-law, and many others. Relationships in an urban cultural context become increasingly complex. However, occupational and associational ties bring people together.

The Church and the Church Planter

Peter Wagner explained that the church can only be as good as the church planter. The church planter is a builder. Building the body of Christ is what ministry is all about; this is what the church planter is called to do. Paul gave specific instructions to church leaders in Ephesians 4:11-14: "And He personally gave some to be apostles, some prophets, some evangelists, some pastors and teachers, for the training of the saints in the work of ministry, to build up the body of Christ."

According to Colossians 2:6-7, "Therefore as you have received Christ Jesus the Lord, walk in Him, rooted and built up in Him and established in the faith, just as you were taught, and overflowing with thankfulness." The planter continues to build, because building lives is an ongoing process. In both 1 Peter 2:5 and Ephesians 2:22, the kingdom of God is described as the building of a house. In other words, the church planter is called to partner with God in the building of the kingdom. The church planter builds a spiritual house by bringing people into relationship with God.[1] The Assemblies of God Church outlines a useful process for church planting. The following steps describe the process of church planting employed by the Assemblies of God Church.

Step 1: Talk with Your Pastor, Mentors, and Other Advisors

Your pastor is in the driver's seat as to when and if he or she may be willing to recommend you as a potential church planter. This can be a gift and a curse, so your maturity will need to be in place for a successful time of training prior to your release to plant.

---

[1] Thomas S. Rainer and Eric Geiger, *Simple Church: Returning to God's Process for Making Disciples* (Nashville: BH Publishing Group, 1995), 110.

If your pastor is willing to recommend you, we would like to have you get a pre-assessment. This will show us where you are weak and where you are strong. The pre-assessment is a wonderful tool for you and your pastor to make a training plan for you.

Step 2: Fill Out the Forms

Have your pastor fill out a recommendation form. You will fill out an application form. If married, the spouse has to fill out a separate copy of the application. Both forms are available on the website.

Step 3: Meet with an Assessment Team

You will be asked to fill out a pre-assessment questionnaire prior to meeting with the assessment team. If married, both spouses need to be present for the assessment. You may be asked to travel to the location of the assessment team, or they may come to you. Either way, you will need to set aside at least six hours for the assessment.

The assessment is not a job interview, nor is it a pass or fail test. The assessment will help you sharpen your understanding of what God calls you to, measure your strengths and weakness, and continue to shape your strategy for planting. The assessment will be reviewed with you, your sending pastor, and the pastor assigned to coach you while planting. This review will determine what you will need to complete in your preparation to plant before you are released.

Step 4: Continue Training

Any preparation or other training will be done at this time. You may still be six months to a year from planting at this point. With the permission of your sending pastor, this is a good time for you to start making contact with the place where you plan to plant a church. Useful information may result from your contacts.

Step 5: Write Your Two-Year Plan

At this time, you may be only three to six months from being released to plant. You will need to have a firm plan in place for the next two years. Your coach and sending pastor can help you with this process. There are also sample plans on the website.

Step 6: Get Official Release Form Signed

This is the time to say goodbye to your current church and hello to the area where you intend to plant. Obtain signatures on your release form. Send the release form to the National Director with a copy to your local church and one for your files. Your local church will start the process of getting signatures, but you will need to follow through in seeing it completed.

Step 7: Plant the Church with the Support of Your Church

Good coaches will ask you the right questions to help you figure out how to plant the church the way God calls you to. Good coaches will help you learn to deal with success as well as disappointment. You should rely on your instincts and prayer to guide you.

Research Implications

The Assemblies of God (AG) embarks on the training of church planters on a continuous basis due to the fact that the mission field is wide with diverse cultures, and ethnic and professional groups.

The work of soul-winning and bringing people back to God could not be achieved without the concerted effort made annually by the church.

On average, the AG starts 275 churches a year. Over the last twenty years, the AG has been the largest international church planting movement with more than 312,000 churches worldwide to date. According to recent reports in "The Church Multiplication Network", the AG is actually one of the few movements to see any growth

over the last few years, averaging about 1 percent each year.

As stated in chapter one of this report, about 17 percent of Americans attend church on a typical Sunday. Between 1990 and 2006, overall church attendance flatlined while the population had a net growth of over 52 million people. Information gathered tells also that to break even or simply maintain a status quo, a church needs to plant at least 3 percent of its total churches each year in order to survive. As long as AG is concerned, thriving and winning the lost is at its very core. AG is passionate about fulfilling the Great Commission. It is important therefore, that every church planter must have at the back of his or her mind to accomplish this objective of moving into the world and preaching the gospel to every creature. New churches must be vigorously planted now and then.

The church planter must acquaint himself or herself with certain key obstacles that have to be overcome if a church plant is to succeed. Common hindrances to a successful church planting are rejection, discouragement, burnout, finances, and spiritual battlefields.

Rejection

Jesus told his disciples in Mathew 10:14, "And whosoever shall not receive you, nor hear your words, when ye depart out of that house or city, shake off the dust of your feet." The church planter must realize from the onset that he or she cannot please everyone, and his or her church may not be attractive to everyone who comes to visit. The church planter undoubtedly has made a strong emotional investment into making the new church. Rejection, both real and perceived, is a fact of life in any congregation; however, it is felt all the more intensely in a new church.

Rejection is especially devastating when someone who has been a part of the core group becomes unhappy and leaves. Many of the people surveyed for this project expressed surprise over the petty things that caused people to pack up and move on. Sometimes it is over the choice of a building site or a small change in the schedule. However, these issues are cumulative; often, a member will leave because a particular situation is the straw that broke the camel's back. There are underlying problems, many of which have nothing to do with the church planter, that cause people to leave.

One problem is that new churches tend to attract individuals who feel a need to exercise control. Perhaps what made them unhappy in their previous churches was their inability to exercise the leadership they felt they should have. A new church with little existing leadership can be quite attractive to such people. But when it becomes apparent that they'll be unable to exercise veto power and that they can't sway the congregation in every decision, even in the new church, they'll look for some excuse to leave and will move on. Whether they sneak out the back or slam the front door, a church planter will still experience the pain of rejection.

The church planter should avoid wallowing in pain and making accusations. Rather, church planters should follow the advice of Jesus, who told His disciples to accept rejection by shaking the dust from their feet and moving on (Mathew 10:14). However, church planters should also do all they can to leave the door open for future contact with those who left the church.

Discouragement

Discouragement is the dangerous weapon of the Devil used to stop the church planter from achieving his or her objective. As the church planter puts in his or her best effort to grow the new congregation, he or she might notice with disappointment that it is not growing as fast as he or she would want. The church planter might begin to wonder whether he or she is doing something wrong and whether God has really called him or her to plant a church. Sometimes, discouragement can come when the church planter loses founding members of the church.

Discouragement will also set in if the church planter begins to compare his or her church to other new churches. Sometimes God blesses a congregation with instant and spectacular growth. This, however, is not the norm, and if church planters think otherwise, they'll quickly become disheartened. Church planters should recognize that every setting and mix of people is unique and focus on celebrating what God is doing.

Burnout

The monotony of responsibility could bring church planters down. It is difficult for a church planter to try to do everything by himself or herself. Burnout is the mental, emotional, and physical exhaustion that can occur when individuals are absorbed in an intense period of work. It is the responsibility of the pastor and church council to balance the needs of the church with the needs of individuals. Church planters need to make sure that everyone has a chance to rest so all can enjoy the fruits of their labors.

Burnout is less likely to occur with church planters when they perform tasks at which they are gifted. Individuals should seek out their gifts and perform them to the best of their abilities.

One of the great safeguards against burnout is teaching people to recognize the way that they have been gifted by the Lord and encouraging them to develop those gifts and areas of ministry.

Finances

The need for money in church planting cannot be overemphasized. Every step a church planter takes involves spending money. The church planter cannot do anything without spending money and should adequately consider finances when planning to open a church. All congregations struggle with finances—that is, if they exercise faith in their approach to ministry, they will always stretch themselves beyond their current resources. Church planters should be realistic in financial planning, seek out solid advice before embarking on major spending, and always involve the congregation in financial issues.

Spiritual Warfare

According to Ephesians 6:12, "For we wrestle not against flesh and blood, but against principalities, against powers, against the rulers of the darkness of this world, against spiritual wickedness in high places." Church planters should not underestimate the power of darkness. They should recognize that church planting is about moving people from the power of darkness into the marvelous light of God. The Devil does not rest and may not be willing to let go. He puts up a fight in different fronts, because he wants to stop the movement of the church.

The church of God must move on anyway, and the kingdom of hell cannot prevail against it. The church planter has the onerous duty of summoning the whole armor of God. Prayer must be made without ceasing. Prayer and fasting are the weapons to fight a spiritual battle. Prayer warriors should be engaged to pray and back up the pastor until victory is won.

Research Applications

The success made in church planting can be credited to the vision of the leaders of the AG organization. It has been noted with interest that the church is managed by intellectuals such as George Wood, who is the General Superintendent, and other professionals like the General Secretary/Treasurer, who has a PhD in engineering, as well as the Assistant General Superintendent, who is a university professor. Vision and training in the area of church planting cannot be traded for anything.

This publication has developed into an area whereby the twenty-first-century church planter can draw strength from ideas developed in this work, which makes the job of church planting less taxing. This research effort is mission-driven and focuses on how to effectively equip through assessing, training, coaching, and strategically positioning the church planter to effectively carry out the onerous task of church planting. The process of achieving the goal of carrying out the Great Commission could be assessed in the form of developing a system, identifying the calling, assessing the system, training, coaching, developing resources, and marketing and communicating.

The discovery system is a set of intentional activities that will help to discover those God has called and connect them with opportunities that will help them clarify and confirm their callings. This system is developed by mentorship. A new church planter is placed to work with an experienced pastor from who he or she can learn how to evangelize and win souls to Christ.

Once a pool of potential planters is identified, the development system will provide pathways for potential planters to work directly with one of hundreds of new churches being planted every year.

As the call of God toward planting a church becomes clearer, it is important for a potential planter to discern where he or she belongs in the church planting process, whether as the lead pastor, team member, or administrative support.

The training system will gather what former church planters have learned and pass this along to the next generation of planters through programs and events like the church multiplication network boot camp.

The church planting process coordinates between districts and parent churches to develop a pool of coaches who can assist potential planters as they journey through all aspects of starting a new church.

The resources development system leverages the scale of the effort to raise funds for the church planter. Traditional and alternative funding opportunities that support new churches and church planting efforts are being harnessed.

The marketing and communications department of the church tells the stories of what God is doing through new churches by providing inspiration, training, and information. This is a vehicle that the church uses to assist planters by creating peer-to-peer networks that facilitate collaboration.

Conclusions

Church planting is God's way of reaching the sinners. God will always use men and women to achieve His objective on earth. People must volunteer their services and be ready to do whatever it takes to do God's work. Definitely, angels cannot do the work of conversion here on earth. In Acts 10, the angel could only visit Cornelius to deliver the message from God but asked him to go to the house of one Simon, a tanner, where Simon Peter was residing. Peter was instructed accordingly to go and present the gospel to Cornelius and his family. The work of conversion and outpouring of the Holy Spirit was done because Peter obeyed and went to the house of the centurion. In order to effectively carry out God's original plan of salvation, there is need for individuals with vision, training, and willingness to plant churches all over North America.

The models described in this chapter stand as examples of churches that were willing to build bridges and reach cross-culturally to others with the gospel. This is a golden era for the church in America. We must have an increasing number of churches that will develop their own guidelines and regulations in order to meet the challenges in their own neighborhoods. The above models create room for variety and freedom of worship in America. Freedom of worship can be enhanced when the barriers posed by cultural distinctions are surmounted with the appropriate church planting strategies.

The church planter ought to understand that today's society is diverse with different cultures and should be equipped to handle the challenges that occur due to urbanization. He or she should put on the whole armor of God, because the mission field can be very hostile. He or she should possess the character and be determined to depend upon God for the success of his or her ministry.

Future Research

Based on the findings of this study, there are numerous recommendations for further study. First, future research should focus on church planting for specific demographic groups. When attempting to establish a new church in an urban area, a church planter should have a body of research upon which he or she can draw to determine how to adapt the new church to local cultural preference. For example, if a church planter is moving into an area with a high blue-collar African American population, research should demonstrate what aspects of church appeal most to that particular demographic group. Of course, research of this nature will never replace communication between the church and the local residents; however, proper research will allow the church planter to gain a more comprehensive understanding of the population the church will serve.

Research should also demonstrate methods to use media technology in church planting in a way that glorifies God. Researchers could conduct a survey that analyzes different churches' experiences and relative success with technology and provide recommendations with regard to the type and quantity of media technology to be used in worship. As noted, media technology appeals to younger generations that the church hopes to court. Therefore, the church should examine how to use technology to appeal to younger generations—yet not in a manner that cheapens or conflicts with the message of God.

Further, research must analyze church plant failure. Much research has focused on successful church plants. However, church planters can learn just as much from failed churches. Quantitative and qualitative research on church plant failure would help church planters to have a more comprehensive understanding of how churches can better respond to their environments and avoid failure.

Finally, there should be additional research that holistically examines demographic shifts in the United States and designs a general church-planting strategy to respond to these changes. This study touched on demographic changes in the United States and considered how these changes might manifest on a micro level in individual churches. However, demographic shifts represent bold, sweeping brush strokes effectively, respond to the objective reality of the urban environment, respond to areas for improvement, and innovate.

Works Cited

Microsoft Encarta Online Encyclopedia. "Jack Kevorkian." http://encarta.msn.com/encyclopedia_761589504/kevorkian.html.

"Enrichment." *A Journal for Pentecostal Ministry*, Spring 2009.

Church Coaching Solutions. "Leadership Coaching." http://www.church-coaching.com/article/coaching for church leaders.

APA Help Center. "Sexual Orientation, Homosexuality and Bisexuality." http://www.apahelpcenter.org/articles/article.php?id=31.

Allen, Roland, *Missionary Methods: St. Paul's or Ours?* Grand Rapids, Michigan: Elderman Publishing, 2006.

Amstutz, Harold E. *Church Planter's Manual.* Cherry Hill, New Jersey: Association of Baptists for World Evangelism, 1985.

Anderson, Leith. *A Church for the Twenty-First Century: Bringing Change to Church to Meet the Challenges of the Changing Society.* Minneapolis, Minnesota: Bethany House Publishers, 1992.

Anderson, Ray. *Minding God's Business.* Pasadena, California: Fuller Seminary Press, 1986.

Barna, George. *The Power of Vision.* Ventura, California: Regal Books, 1992.

Barna, George. *User Friendly Churches.* Ventura, California: Regal Books, 1991.

Becker, Paul. *Dynamic Church Planting.* Vista, California: Multiplication Ministries, 1992.

Benjamin, Dick. *The Church Planter's Handbook.* S. Lake Tahoe, California: Christian Equippers International, 1988.

Bosch, David J. *Transforming Mission: Paradigm Shifts in the Theology of Mission.* New York: Orbis Books, 1994.

Boydston, Bradley L. *Getting Started, A Church Planting Handbook for Laypeople.* Turlock, California: Bradley L. Boydston, 1996.

Brock, Charles. *The Principles and Practice of Indigenous Church Planting.* Nashville: Broadman Press, 1976.

Brown, Peter. *The Cult of the Saints: Its Rise and Function in Latin Christianity.* Chicago: University of Chicago Press, 1982.

Bunch, David T., and Barbara L. Oden. *Multi-housing Congregations: How to Start and Grow Congregations in Multi-housing Communities.* Atlanta: Home Mission Board, 1991.

Burton, Laurel A. *Pastoral Paradigms: Christian Ministry in a Pluralistic Culture.* Washington, DC: The Alban Institute, 1988.

Chaney, Charles L. *Church Planting and the End of the Twentieth Century.* Wheaton, Illinois: Tyndale House, 1991.

Christine, Stuart, and Martin Robinson. *Planting Tomorrow's Church Today: A Comprehensive Handbook.* Turnbridge Wells, UK: Monarch Publications, 1992.

Conn, Harvie. *Planting and Growing Urban Churches: From Dream to Reality.* Grand Rapids: Baker Book House, 1997.

Countryman, L. William. *Good News of Jesus.* Boston: Trinity Press International, 1993.

Coursey, Caylan. *How Churches Can Start Churches.* Nairobi, Kenya: Baptist Publications House, 1984.

Ellis, Roger, and Roger Mitchell. *Radical Church Planting.* Wheaton, Illinois: Crossway Books, 1992.

Estep, Michael R., ed. *The Great Commission Church Planting Strategy.* Kansas City, Missouri: Nazarene Publishing House, 1988.

Faircloth, Samuel D. *Church Planting for Reproduction.* Grand Rapids: Baker Book House, 1991.

Feeney, James, H. *Church Planting by the Team Method.* Anchorage, Alaska: Abbott Loop Christian Center, 1988.

Filson, Floyd V. "The Significance of the Early House Churches." *Journal of Literature* 58 (1939): 109–112.

Fries, Heinrich. *Fundamental Theology.* Washington, DC: The
Catholic University of America Press, 1996.

Fries, Heinrich. *Fundamental Theology.* Washington, DC: The
Catholic University of America Press, 1996.

George, Carl F. *Prepare Your Church for the Future.* Tarrytown,
New York: Fleming H. Revell Co., 1991.

Gibbs, Eddie, and Ryan K. Bolger. *Emerging Churches, Creating
Christian Community in Postmodern Cultures.* Grand Rapids:
Baker Academic, 2006.

Godwin, David, F. *Church Planting Methods.* DeSoto, Texas:
Lifeshare Communications, 1984.

Greenway, Roger S., ed. *Guidelines for Urban Church Planting.*
Grand Rapids: Baker Book House, 1976.

Handy, Robert T. A History of the Churches in the United States
and Canada. New York: Oxford University Press, 1977.

Hedlund, Roger. *The Mission of the Church in the World.* Grand
Rapids: Baker Book House, 1991.

Hesselgrave, David, J. *Planting Churches Cross-Culturally: North
America and Beyond.* Grand Rapids: Baker Book House, 1980.

Hill, Monica, ed. *How to Plant Churches.* London: MARC Europe, 1984.

Hsu, Albert Y. *The Suburban Christian.* Downers Grove, Illinois:
InterVarsity Press, 2006.

Hunter, George G. *To Spread the Power: Church Growth in the
Wesleyan Spirit.* Nashville: Abingdon Press, 1987.

Kane, J. Herbert. *Christian Missions in Biblical Perspective.* Grand
Rapids: Baker Book House, 1976.

Kimball, Dan. *The Emerging Church.* Grand Rapids: Zondervan,
2005.

Kunz, Marilyn. *How to Start a Neighborhood Bible Study.* New
York: Neighborhood Bible Studies, 1966.

Lehman, James H. *Thank God for New Churches.* Elgin, Illinois:
Brethren Press, 1984.

Lewis, Larry L. *The Church Planter's Handbook.* Nashville:
Broadman Press, 1992.

Livingstone, Greg. *Planting Churches in Muslim Cities*. Grand Rapids: Baker Book House, 1993.

Logan, Robert E., and Jeff Rast. *International Church Planting Guide*. Alta Loma, California: Strategic Ministries, Inc., 1988.

Malphurs, Aubrey. *Planting Growing Churches for the 21st Century: A Comprehensive Guide for New Churches and Those Desiring Renewal*. Grand Rapids: Baker Book Club, 1992.

Mannoia, Kevin W. *Church Planting: The Next Generation*. Indianapolis: Lite and Life, 1996.

Marsden, George M. *Religion and American Culture*. Independence, Kentucky: Cengage Learning, 2000.

McGavran, Donald A. *Effective Evangelism: A Theological Mandate*. Phillipsburg, New Jersey: Presbyterian and Reformed, 1988.

Meeks, Wayne A. *The First Urban Christians*. New Haven: Yale University Press, 1983.

Murray, Stuart and Lings, George. *Church Planting: Past and Future (Evangelism)*. Harrisonburg, Virginia: Herald Press, 2003.

Nevius, John L. *Planting and Development of Missionary Churches*. Nutley, New Jersey: Presbyterian and Reformed, 1958.

Nicholson, Steve. *Coaching Church Planters: A Manual for Church Planters and Those Who Coach Them*. Stafford, Texas: Association of Vineyard Churches USA, 2008.

Nikkel, James. *Antioch Blueprints: A Manual of Church Planting Information and Church Growth Strategies*. Winnipeg, Manitoba: Canadian Conference of Mennonite Brethren Churches, 1987.

Olson, David T. *The American Church in Crisis*. Grand Rapids: Zondervan, 2008.

Payne, J. D. *Discovering Church Planting: An Introduction to the Whats, Whys, and Hows of Global Church Planting*. Nottingham, UK: Paternoster, 2009

Rahner, Karl. *Foundations of Christian Faith*, Translated by William V. Dych. New York: Crossroad Publishing Co., 1994.

Rainer, Thomas S., and Eric Geiger. *Simple Church: Returning to God's Process for Making Disciples.* Nashville: B & H Publishing Group, 2008.

Redford, Jack. *Planting New Churches.* Nashville: Broadman Press, 1978.

Reed, James E., and Ronnie Prevost. *A History of Christian Education.* Nashville: Broadman and Holman, 1949.

Robinson, Martin and Christine Stuart. *Planting Tomorrow's Churches Today.* Speldhurst, United Kingdom: Monarch Publications, 1992.

Stetzer, Ed. *Planting New Churches in a Postmodern Age.* Nashville: Broadman Press, 2003.

Stetzer, Ed. *Planting Missional Churches.* Nashville: B & H Academic, 2006

Shenk, David W. and Ervin R. Stutzman. *Creating Communities in the Kingdom: New Testament Models of Church Planting.* Scottdale, Pennsylvania: Herald Press, 1988.

Smith, Sid, ed. *Church Planting in the Black Community.* Nashville: Convention Press, 1989.

Starr, Timothy. *Church Planting: Always in Season.* Guelph, Ontario: Fellowship of Evangelical Baptist Churches of Canada, 1978.

Stetzer, Ed. *Planting New Churches in a Postmodern Age.* Nashville: BH Publishing Group, 2003.

Strategies for Church Growth: Tools for Effective Mission and Evangelism. Ventura, California: Regal Books, 1994.

Sullivan, Bill M. *Ten Steps to Breaking the 200 Barrier.* Kansas City, Missouri: Beacon Hill Press, 1988.

Tidsworth, Floyd. *Life Cycle of a New Congregation.* Nashville: Broadman Press, 1992.

Tinsley, William C. *Upon This Rock: Dimensions of Church Planting.* Atlanta: Home Mission Board, 1985.

Towns, Elmer L. and Douglas Porter. *Churches That Multiply: A Bible Study on Church Planting.* Kansas City, Missouri: Beacon Hill Press, 2000.

Towns, Elmer L. *Getting a Church Started*. Lynchburg, Virginia: Church Growth Institute, 1985.

Underwood, Charles M. *Planting the Independent Fundamental Church (Pastors Tell How to Do it Successfully)*. Greenville, South Carolina: Bob Jones University, 1972.

Wagner, Peter C. *Church Planting for a Greater Harvest*. Ventura, California: Regal Books, 1990.

Wagner, Peter C., and Donald A. McGavran. *Understanding Church Growth*. Grand Rapids: William B. Eerdmans Publishing Company, 1991.

Walker, Peter. *In the Steps of Jesus*. Grand Rapids: Zondervan, 2006.

Warren, Rick. *The Purpose Driven Church*. Grand Rapids: Zondervan, 1995.

Waterman, Leonard. *A Manual for Starting New Churches*. Wheaton, Illinois: Conservative Baptist HMS, 1983.

Wiersbe, Warren W. *The Joy of Preaching*. Grand Rapids: Kregel Publications, 1989.

Wilson, Paul Scott. *A Concise History of Preaching*. Nashville: Abingdon, 1992.

Winter, Ralph D., and Steven C. Hawthorne. *Perspectives on the World Christian Movement: A Reader*. Pasadena, California: William Carey Library, 1992.

Wuthnow, Robert. *Christianity in the 21st Century: Reflections on the Challenges*. NY: Oxford University Press, 1993.

Wuthnow, Robert. *Growing Up Religious Christians and Jews and Their Journeys of Faith*. Boston: Beacon Press, 2000.

Yount, David. *The Future of Christian Faith in America*. New York: Macmillan Press, 2004.

Appendix

Other Models of Specific Churches

Planting Cases

From Dr. Roger Greenway's seminar on Urban Strategies, the following models are added for further consideration (Greenway 1991).

Model Number One: Building First

1. Erect or buy a building, and set out to fill it.
2. An old method
3. Often a failure
4. Still used and is successful in high receptive places (i.e., East Africa)

Model Number Two: Multi-congregational Church

1. Designed for ethnically pluralistic cities
2. Unity and diversity
3. Economy and mutual support (figure 9)

Note: This approach is different from the landlord/tenant arrangement in which ethnic congregations make use of building facilities owned by churches to which they do not become a vital part.

Model Number Three: Fellowship Center Model or Ministry

1. Neutral location
2. Non-threatening
3. Nondenominational image
4. Usually charismatic
5. Tend to grow large
6. Known for excellent music, teaching
7. Some are denominationally liked, but it's not emphasized.
8. Broad appeal

An identifiable church emerges.
In many cities, this produces the largest churches.